Midwest Corn Fusion

A Collection of Recipes & Humor

by

James McCaffrey

© 2006 Jim McCaffrey
First printing December 2006

Cover photograph by Larsh Bristol
Back cover photograph of Jim McCaffrey by Erik Berg
Cover design by Erik Berg

ISBN: 0-9778339-0-9

This book is dedicated to
Angela McCaffrey, the late Isaac Seymour, and the late Larsh Bristol

Introduction

I started out as a child. No! Wait a minute, wrong book. Actually, I started out writing this book about how the various cuisines of the numerous ethnic groups that have settled in the Midwest have melded together. Well, little of that happened. The final composition ended up being recipes of my own, recipes we created, different family recipes that have been passed down from generation to generation, and recipes from around the Midwest that just begged to be included. Believe me, there was some major pleading going on.

Seriously, I just wanted to share home, friend and restaurant recipes that I have gathered over time. I purposely have tried to keep this project on a humorous and light side (mostly). I get one of my greatest enjoyments by cooking and serving food to friends and family. We made the recipes in this book primarily on weekends. It wasn't unusual for 20 - 25 people to show up to say hi and enjoy whatever was on the menu. Great sounding board when you have that many opinions.

I did my best to keep the recipes fairly easy to make and with ingredients that are almost always available. A few ingredients, such as Morel mushrooms, may be a little more difficult to obtain. Don't be afraid to substitute for items you don't have. The whole idea is to have fun and enjoy with family and friends and not stress out because it was a bad year for zucchini. Always try to use fresh products if available, but if not, substitute frozen or dried. Canned will work, but that would be my last choice, especially for vegetables.

O.K., enough lecturing. I want to tell you this has been all and all a wonderful experience. We had a blast making up all of these recipes. We didn't have a clue as to what we were getting into as far as writing a book, and that was a struggle at times, but in the end, we accomplished finishing the project in way less than record time.

The we I'm talking about are all the wonderful people who in some way or another made a contribution to this book. First, my sister Angie McCaffrey Cosimini, who is the inspiration for writing this book to start with. Five years ago, she was diagnosed with Stage 4 Ovarian cancer. She took on the challenge of the deadly disease and beat the odds. She went into remission for four years. It came back again this year and she has gone through all of the struggle and once more has beaten the odds. Her attitude is tremendous and makes one know that if you put your mind to it, you can accomplish the impossible. Thanks Angie.

Next, I'd like to thank my wife Brenda for her support and help. We had lots of cleaning up to do weekend after weekend. I'd like to thank and acknowledge the rest of my immediate family, Shanon Benson and Morgan Tobin and their son Kamran, Craig Witt, Fawn Benson and their son August, and Conor McCaffrey. I'd especially like to thank Craig, Fawn and Morgan. Craig got the computer set up and took care of technical problems. Fawn spent a lot of time typing in introductions and material. Morgan did a lot of editing. Fawn, Shanon, Morgan, Craig and Conor all helped cooking and coming up with recipes.

Next, I'd like to thank Erik Berg who made the cover and the back for the book. The scene on the cover was a picture taken by Larsh Bristol and I'd like to thank Larsh for letting us use it. I'd like to thank Jason Schwarz for spending a few of his free hours on Sundays editing the book for me. Jason, you did a great job. A big thanks also to Deb Paulson who gave us the big help we needed at the end to get ready for printing.

Lastly, I'd like to thank the following people who contributed through various means like taste testing, recipes, making connections, and generally just being wonderful people and helping out. (There is no particular order to this). Barry (The Mustard Man) and Patty Levenson, Bruce Pierce, the Family of Ike Seymour, Mark and Owen Burgdorf, Bruce and Pam Butters, Mike Domine, Nate Leistikow, Charley Cosimini, Terry Jacobson, Annette Oswald, Erik Olson, Tom Tofte, Murray and Khrista Linnevold, Pam Taylor and Buzz Thomas, John and Marcy Miller, Lindsay and Lee Lee, Jeff and Darlene Martin, Bruce and Lynn Kuennen, Jerry and Cheryl Lenguadoro, Ignacio, Don and Lousie Fleckinger, Clayton Snyder, Judy Treloar, Don and Carol Nelson, Karla Hoppin, Amy Wilkinson, Laura and Randy Ellingson, Jane and Leon Bullerman, Mark and Joannie Smeby, Dana Spry, Clair Kunz, Billy Kunz.

Thanks to Bruce Butters who helped do a final edit, and the folks at Whitehall Printing who were great at getting this together for us. Thanks Sandra.

If I've forgotten anybody, it certainly wasn't intentional.

Table of Contents

1. Spicing Up Norway — 13
2. Cheeseheads, Cheddarheads, and Giant Mice — 27
3. The Mighty Yellow Condiment — 39
   (Or Do You Know The Mustard Man?)
4. Salad Daze — 51
5. Mushroom Mania — 65
6. Flim Flamming at the Farmers Market — 77
7. BBQ Chapter: Big Daddy Lives in Our Hearts Forever — 89
8. Little Italy — 101
9. Grin and Beer It — 113
10. State Dish of Minnesota — 125
11. Waiter, There's a Fly in My Soup — 137
12. Party Favors — 149
13. Midwest Americana — 161
14. Just Desserts — 173
15. What Goes On in the Cornfield, Stays in the Cornfield! — 185

Spicing Up Norway

I grew up Irish German Catholic in a Norwegian Lutheran Community. I mean, what kind of a country is this, anyway? I started working at one of the local grocery stores when I was in high school, bagging groceries, stocking shelves, and unloading delivery trucks. When the Christmas holiday season rolled around, we would receive wooden crates filled with dried cod soaking in lye. (And that's no lie.) This is a Norwegian delicacy called lutefisk served traditionally during the Christmas season with boiled potatoes and canned green peas. It's kind of like a jellied fish clump which is spiced up by pouring bacon fat over it. It's the gastronomic event of the year, so you can imagine what the rest of the year is like. (Just remember when they outlaw lutefisk, only the outlaws will have lutefisk.)

This chapter contains recipes that I have created and/or shared over the years with my Norwegian friends that have a little kick to them. Most have said, "mange tak," (many thanks). Others have just run down the street yelling obscenities about an Irish cook who has just challenged their taste buds.

UFF DA!

Shrimp Creole

We have a one-day festival in Decorah on the last Saturday of August every year called "Live On Winnebago." Winnebago St. is closed off and everyone gathers to celebrate, shop, dance, and eat. It's a grand affair that local resident, Scott, got going to do something positive for our community. An all-day extravaganza with live music and bands from as far away as Africa, artists displaying their wonderful crafts, face painting, kids games, and of course, food. There are seven to nine vendors of totally different ethnic foods, so it is a treat to eat. Chicken Creole is one of the dishes we serve up.

The following recipe is a version of this dish using shrimp as it's main attraction.

(serves 6-8)

- 2 tbls. olive oil
- 8 oz. fresh mushrooms, slice
- 2 celery stalks, chopped
- 1 green pepper, chopped
- 1 large onion, chopped
- 10 garlic cloves, minced
- 2 jalapeno peppers, stemmed seeded and diced

- 1 tbl. Creole seasoning
- 1 tsp. red pepper
- 3-14 1/2 oz. cans Mexican stewed tomatoes
- 1-28 oz. can crushed tomatoes
- 1 lb. hot Italian sausages, grilled/ fried, and sliced into 1/4 inch slices
- 1 1/2 lbs. uncooked shrimp shelled and deveined

Heat oil in a large heavy-bottomed skillet on medium heat. Add all vegetables and stir fry for about 5 minutes or until the mushrooms begin to lose their water. Add spices and mix thoroughly. Add crushed and stewed tomatoes including juice and hot Italian sausage slices. Bring to a simmer for about 15 minutes. Add shrimp. Watch carefully. As soon as shrimp turns pink, it is done. Serve immediately over cooked rice.

Mac's Cajun Sizzlers

My good friends, Tom and Theresa, own a great bar in Decorah named "Your Place." Once a year we have a three-day festival called Nordic Fest, which brings out the best of our predominately Norwegian community. We try to do our part in contributing to the cause by offering the masses an alternative to lutefisk and lefse. Tom asked me to come up with a spicy/hot/oh-my-god-my-pants-are-on-fire! type of bratwurst/sausage. And here is what I created.

I have another wonderful friend, John, who is the meat manager at a local grocery store in Decorah. He mixed this up for us and put it into casings. If you don't have this availability or a mixer with a sausage stuffer, just make patties. Be sure to have lots of cooling refreshments on hand and maybe even a fire extinguisher.

6 Brats or Patties	200 Brats or Patties
1/2 medium onion, skinned	24 onions, skinned
4-6 garlic cloves, peeled	140-180 garlic cloves, peeled
4 good sized jalepenos, destemmed	140 jalapenos, destemmed
5 tsp. Cajun seasoning	60 tbl. Cajun seasoning
1 tsp. red cayenne pepper	4 tbl. red cayenne pepper
2 lbs. ground pork	70 lbs. ground pork
Casing (if used)	Casing (if used)

Puree onion, garlic, and jalapeno peppers in a food processor or blender. Thoroughly mix with seasonings and ground pork. Stuff into casing or make patties. There is a lot of moisture in this mixture. Don't worry, however; it will cook out on the grill. Also, since it is pork, make sure you cook it until 165 degrees or no longer pink inside.

Chicken and Sausage Gumbo

Here is my version of this classic, down-home Louisiana, one-pot cookery. If andouille sausage is not available, just substitute some hot Italian sausage or Polish kielsaba, depending on what your taste for hotness is. I like to serve some good garlic bread with this dish for mopping up.

- 1 1/2 lbs. mushrooms, sliced
- 2 green peppers, chopped
- 4 stalks celery, chopped
- 8-10 garlic cloves, minced
- 3 medium onions, chopped
- 2 gal. water
- 1 gal. chicken broth
- 4 lbs. andouille sausage links, cooked & sliced thin
- 5-6 lbs. cooked chicken breast, diced (season with cajun seasoning)
- Cajun seasoning
- Salt
- Fresh ground black pepper
- 1 1/2 lbs. butter
- 3 cups flour
- 5 cans (14 oz.) rotel tomatoes and green chiles
- 1 (29 oz.) can diced tomatoes

In a very large pot put mushrooms, water and chicken broth, bring to a boil, then let simmer. Chop, mince, and dice veggies and meats. In a large skillet melt butter at med- low heat. Add flour to make a roux. Stir constantly 10-15 minutes. The roux will turn golden brown and have nutty flavor. Add veggies and saute 3-4 minutes. Add sausage and chicken. Put mixture in a larger pot, add water, chicken broth, green chiles and tomatoes & bring to a boil. Gumbo will thicken. Taste and add cajun seasoning, salt & fresh ground pepper to taste. Enjoy! Serves 30 to 40. For a smaller crowd just cut in half or quarter.

Fish Tacos

My good friend, Craig, was over at my house one weekend and asked if I had ever made fish tacos. I said no, but it sounds like a worthwhile endeavor. So, I did a little research, combined a couple of interesting ideas and the following is what we came up with. I think you will have a great time treating your friends with this.

(serves 4)

1-12 oz. can evaporated milk
8 limes
2 large tomatoes, chopped
1 medium red onion, chopped
3 garlic cloves, minced
1 green pepper, chopped
2 jalapeno peppers, deseeded and diced
Salt and pepper

Fresh cilantro (optional)
2 cups peanut or corn oil
1 1/2 lbs. white fish (haddock, cod, etc)
2 cups white flour
3 tbl. Cajun seasoning
1/2 head small red cabbage shredded
20 corn tortillas

In a small bowl combine evaporated milk and the juice of 7 limes. Let stand at room temperature at least 30 minutes. Divide in half.

Combine the juice of the remaining lime, tomatoes, garlic, green- and jalapeno peppers and fresh cilantro, chopped (if desired). Salt and pepper to taste. This is fresh salsa. Set aside.

Heat oil to 360 degrees in a heavy duty skillet. Check temperature with a candy thermometer. Do not overheat or oil might burn.

Cut fish into 1/2 X 2 inch strips. Combine cajun seasoning and flour. Dip fish pieces into half of the lime milk, dredge in flour, and fry in oil until lightly brown on all sides. Drain on paper towels. Warm tortillas one at a time, flipping in 10 to 15 seconds, over medium heat in a dry, heavy duty skillet until flexible—about 30 to 40 seconds altogether. Top tortillas with 2 to 3 fish pieces, cabbage, a little remaining lime milk and fresh salsa. Eat and be happy!

Fresh Salsa & Chips

This is always a hit when you have a crowd of people over for brunch, watching a game or just having a cocktail.
If you like your salsa hotter, just leave the seeds and veins of the jalepenos in. I like to serve this with some really cold Mexican beer, like Dos Equis or Corona with a little lime.

- 3 to 4 lbs. fresh ripe tomatoes, diced into small pieces
- 1 large red onion, diced fine
- 1 large green pepper, diced fine
- 4 to 6 garlic cloves, minced
- 4 to 6 jalapeno peppers, deveined, deseeded and diced fine
- 2 limes
- Salt
- Coarse ground black pepper
- Tortilla chips of your choice

You can put this together right away in the container that you are serving the salsa in. Just make sure the bowl is large enough to hold all of the ingredients and there is enough room to mix. Combine the tomatoes, onion, green pepper, garlic, and jalapeno peppers. Slice limes in half. Use a fork to help squeeze out the lime juice by twisting on the lime pulp (called forking the lime). Add this to the salsa and stir. Now add salt and pepper to taste. I like to refrigerate the salsa for a couple of hours. It really helps the different flavors to meld together. For hotter salsa, don't devein or deseed the jalepenos.

Pork and Green Chile Empanadas

We have a wonderful nursery about 10 miles north of Decorah called Willowglen. The owners, Lindsay and Lee, decided to have a seminar and fall sale and asked us if we could make up some on-hand food for the participants. Lindsay thought that empanadas would be a nice touch. They are something different and are not readily available in Northeast Iowa. I was a little hesitant, having never made them before, but I'm always up for a challenge. We made a total of 300 pork and green chile, vegetarian, and apple cinnamon empanadas. We couldn't hand them out fast enough and sold out in an hour. Needless to say, they were a hit. Here is our pork and green chile recipe.

Filling

- 2 lbs. ground pork
- 6 green chiles or a 4 oz. can green chiles
- 6 garlic cloves, minced
- 1 med. yellow onion, diced
- 1 tbl. Cajun seasoning

Dough

- 8 cups unbleached white flour
- 1/2 cup vegetable shortening or lard
- 3-4 cups chicken broth

Brown ground pork and drain. If using fresh green chiles, either hold with a tongs over an open stove flame or use a grille, searing the skin until it starts to blacken or bubble on all sides. Throw into a paper bag for twenty minutes and let cool. The skin will peel right off. Deseed, destem and mince. Combine fresh/canned chiles, onion, garlic, and Cajun seasoning with the ground pork. Set aside.

Put flour into a large mound on a counter top. Make a pocket in the center and pour in 1 cup chicken broth. Mix in and continue this process until dough is no longer dry. If you think it is too wet add a little more flour. Add shortening and knead until mixed well. Shape dough into golf ball sized rounds. If you have a tortilla press, great; however two heavy books can also accomplish the next step. Cut a gallon food storage bag down its sides. Place in tortilla press opened up like a book. Put one dough ball in the center of the press and close press. Open press and take plastic bag out. Remove flattended dough and place on a lightly floured surface. Put 1-2 large tablespoons of the pork filling in the center of the dough. Fold over in half. Crimp the edges with a fork. Place on baking sheet. Repeat until all dough is filled. Bake in a 350 degree oven about 20 minutes until crust is golden brown. Serve immediately.

Lamb Stew with Jalapenos and Green Chiles

Try this out for a different way to take a walk on the wild side. Make sure to use the freshest lamb you can find. This dish serves well with a hearty red wine such as Cabernet Sauvignon or Zinfandell. Lip-smacking good!

(serves 6-8)

- 3 lbs. boneless lamb shoulder cut into 2" cubes
- 1 cup flour
- 3 tsp. oregano (Mexican, preferably)
- Salt and pepper to taste
- Peanut or corn oil
- 1 large yellow onion, chopped
- 6 green chiles or 1-4oz can diced green chiles
- 4 jalapeno peppers, stems removed and diced fine
- 6 cloves garlic, crushed and minced
- 3 large tomatoes, diced
- 6 cups beef broth
- 2 large carrots peeled and sliced into 1/4" pieces
- 4 large potatoes peeled and cut into 3/4" cubes
- Salt and pepper

Mix flour, oregano, salt, and pepper. Dredge lamb cubes in flour mixture. Heat 3 tbl. oil in a large heavy dutch oven. Brown lamb cubes on all sides at medium heat. Add a little more oil if necessary. Remove lamb and set aside. If using fresh green chiles, hold with a tongs over an open flame or use a grille and sear until skin begins to blacken on all sides. Place in paper bag and let cool 20 minutes. Deskin, destem, deseed, and dice. Put chiles, onion, jalepenos, and garlic in the same pan and add a little more oil if needed. Saute 3-4 minutes on medium heat until onion becomes translucent. Add broth and lamb. Simmer 45 minutes, stirring occasionally. Add tomatoes, carrots, and potatoes, again stirring occasionally. Simmer about 30 minutes or so, until potatoes are tender. Season to taste with salt and pepper..

Chicken with 40 Cloves of Garlic

Don't let the amount of garlic scare you off. This is absolutely marvelous. I like to bake or toast some slices of french bread at the same time, and when the chicken is cooked, the garlic cloves can be squeezed onto the toast and spread like butter. Add a little salt if you like.

(serves 4)

1-3 1/2 lb. cut up chicken
1 cup olive oil
2 large carrots, peeled and sliced thin
4 celery stalks, sliced thin
Salt and pepper

40 cloves garlic, unpeeled
1 cup dry white wine
Juice of 1 large lemon
1 bunch fresh parsley
1 loaf rustic french bread sliced into rounds

Wash chicken and pat dry with paper towels. Coat with olive oil and brown on all sides in a heavy duty skillet. Place on paper towels to absorb excess oil. In a large metal casserole, spread out carrots and celery. Salt and pepper chicken to taste on one side. Place that side down in casserole on top of carrots and celery. Salt and pepper to taste the remaining side. Stuff garlic cloves in and around chicken. Cover tightly with heavy duty aluminum foil. Bake at 375 degrees for 30-40 minutes until chicken juices run clear. When chicken is about done, place french bread slices on a cookie sheet and put into oven to toast (about ten minutes). Pull out when toasted brown. When chicken is ready, take out of oven and place on platter with garlic to one side. Cover and keep warm. Place casserole on top of stove, add wine and simmer. Scrape bottom of pan (deglaze) and reduce wine to 1/2. Add lemon juice and reduce a little more. Divvy up chicken on plates. Pour some sauce over and garnish with parsley. Squeeze garlic cloves on toast.

Shrimp Diablo

The secret to making great shrimp is to make sure that it is not overcooked. As soon as shrimp begins to turn pink, remove from the heat and serve immediately. Personally, I like to spice this sauce up a little more, but not everybody enjoys that pleasure as much as I. So don't be afraid to have some red pepper flakes on hand to pass around. That way, everyone can enjoy this dish at their own desired heat.

(serves 6-8)

- 6 cloves garlic, minced
- 1 tbl. olive oil
- 6 green chiles (roasted, skinned, stemmed, seeds removed, chopped) OR 1-4 oz. can diced green chiles
- 1 medium red onion, diced
- 2-28 oz. cans crushed tomatoes
- 8-10 turns black pepper mill
- 2-3 pinches red pepper flakes
- Salt 1 lb. thin spaghetti noodles
- 1 1/2 lb. (30-40) uncooked shrimp, peeled and deveined
- 1 oz. fresh basil, chopped
- Fresh grated Romano cheese for topping

In a large skillet saute garlic for 2 minutes. Add chiles, tomatoes, black and red pepper. Simmer for 1 hour, stirring occasionally. When sauce is 15 minutes away from being done, cook noodles according to package directions and drain. Add shrimp and basil when sauce has 3-5 minutes to go. When shrimp turns pink, turn off heat and serve immediately over noodles. Pass around the Romano!

Chef's note: It helps to have noodle water ready ahead of time. Bring to a boil while sauce is simmering and shut off until needed.

Fire in the Hole Sirloin Wrap

Although this dish is from Southwest USA and Northern Mexico, it has graced our table on several occasions. This is not for the meek of hotness. We served it for Christmas one year and some of my in-laws debated on just how slow of a death they could inflict on me! Serve these with some refried beans and rice which offset the heat. This is my version of a recipe found in *The Border Cookbook* by Cheryl and Bill Jamison (great cookbook!).

(serves 8-10)

- 3 lbs. boneless sirloin, sliced across the grain into 1/8" strips
- 12 tbl. Safflower or corn oil
- 12 tbl. soy sauce
- 4 tbl. dried Mexican oregano
- 6-8 garlic cloves, minced
- 2 tbl. safflower or corn oil
- 2 large white onions, sliced thin
- 8-10 green chiles roasted, destemmed, skinned and diced (You can substitute 3 4oz. cans diced green chiles, but it won't be as hot)
- 3 large fresh tomatoes, halved and sliced thin
- 12-10" flour tortillas warmed
- 3 cups fresh salsa (see page 18)

Marinate sirloin 12-24 hours with 12 tbl. oil, soy sauce, oregano and garlic. Drain. Warm remaining oil in large heavy skillet over high heat and saute sirloin in 3-4 batches until browned. Set aside. Saute onions, tomatoes, and chiles over medium heat until onions are soft. Stir in sirloin. Fill tortillas, top with fresh salsa and let the party begin.

Chef's note: To roast chilies, hold and turn over a open flame or on a bbq grille until chiles begin to blister and blacken. Place immediately in a paper bag for 15-20 minutes. Let cool and skin should pull right off.

Red Chile Sauce/Salsa Verde

Here are 2 basic Tex/Mex sauces I think come in very handy, they are easy to make when you have a little extra time on your hands.

Red Chile Sauce

3 tbl. peanut oil
2 cloves garlic, minced
1/2 tsp. Mexican oregano
2 tbl. flour

1/2 cup red chili powder (preferably New Mexican)
2 cups beef or chicken broth
Salt

Heat oil in medium sauce pan. Saute garlic and oregano 2 minutes. Add flour and whisk over medium heat about 4 minutes. Turn heat. Add chili powder and whisk 30 seconds. Stir in broth to desired thickness. Makes 2-2 1/2 cups

Salsa Verde

2 small jalapeno peppers, chopped
12 fresh tomatillos, husks removed
1 med onion, quartered
2 cloves garlic, minced

1/4 cup fresh cilantro, chopped
1 tsp. extra virgin olive oil
1 tbl. lime juice
Salt and fresh ground black pepper to taste

Halve tomatillos. Add to food processor and pulse 3-4 times. Add remaining ingredients and blend. Adjust seasoning and chill. Makes 2 cups.

My Favorite Irish Joke

Patrick and Mary had been married for years. It was Patrick's birthday. When he got home from work Mary informed him that she had made his favorite meal.

"Oh," asked Patrick, "Did you make lobster?"

"Oh yes, Patrick," said Mary.

"And those little red potatoes?" queried Patrick.

"Oh yes," said Mary.

"And julienned carrots?" asked Patrick.

"Of course," said Mary.

"And snails? Did you make snails?" Patrick asked.

"Oh my word Patrick, I forgot the snails. I'll run right down to the market and get some." said Mary.

"No, no, no," Patrick replied. "You've been cooking all day, I'll run and get them myself."

"All right," said Mary, "But don't you be stopping by the pub on the way!"

Patrick said, "No, I'll be right back."

So Patrick runs to the store and picks up a sack of snails. On his way back, he comes across Mikey standing in front of the pub. Mikey says, "Patrick, it's your birthday, let me buy you a pint."
Patrick says, "No, I promised Mary I'd be right back."
Mikey says, "In the time we've been talking, we could have quaffed one down."
Patrick says, "Oh, all right." So Mikey buys Patrick one and Patrick buys Mikey one. They keep at it for a couple of hours.

Patrick suddenly grabs his sack of snails and says, "Mary is going to be furious," and races home.

Just as he gets to his house, the bottom of the bag falls out and the snails fall to the sidewalk. Mary comes to the door and yells "Patrick, where have you been?"

Patrick crouches down and gesturing to the snails says, "Move along laddies, move along."

Cheeseheads, Cheddarheads & Giant Mice

Something tells me, Dorothy, we're not in Kansas anymore. No, we're in the land where people wear green and gold jerseys with a number 4 on them to church on sundays. Vince, Bart, and Brett are institutions with no last names. Friday night fish fries and a couple/two-three beers are considered to be an unalienable right (rite?). Fleet Farm is a shoppers mecca. Beer and bratwurst are revered like champagne and caviar. What is this enchanting land? It is, of course, Wisconsin, home to 126 wonderful cheese factories. If you are driving down the road and you see a 20 foot mouse sitting by the side of the road, you will know you have located one of these factories. Wisconsin is the number-one cheese producing state in the USA. However at the time of this writing, there is a state out there trying to Californicate that title. Most of the operations are small and a lot are cooperatives made up of local farmers. But they have commandeered a multitude of national and international awards for their craft. Not bad for a state whose residents saw the movie "Fargo" and didn't hear an accent.

"Hey, who cut the cheese?"

Parmesan Crisps

Your friends will think you are a culinary genius with this very simple treat. Make sure you don't overcook the cheese, as it tends to get a little bitter when well done. You can get creative and form different shapes as long as the cheese is still warm and pliable. Always remember to be careful because you are dealing with hot food.

16 ounces fine grated Parmesan cheese

Preheat oven to 325 degrees. Using a couple of cookie sheets, sprinkle cheese into 3-4 inch circles. Try not to get it piled too high or it will cook unevenly. Sprinkle is the key word here. When it cooks, you want it to come out looking like lattice work. You might want to experiment a little by making just one or two and baking them until you get the right proportion figured out. It is pretty easy. Pop into preheated oven for 4-5 minutes. Pull out before the cheese begins to brown. Basically, it just needs to melt. Let cool and using a spatula, transfer to a plate. Repeat until all cheese is cooked. These are great to have around as an hors d'oeuvre or as a garnish for items like mashed potatoes. If you want to get creative, while cheese is still warm, you can drape them over shot glasses or something similar to make little food baskets. (See *Tulip Teacups For Pat* page 150).

Wisconsin Beer Cheese Soup

Leave it to the cheeseheads to come up with the marriage of two of the best products they make in the state. Believe it or not, the traditional topping for this soup is fresh popped popcorn. That will get a few heads shaking at your next food festivity.

(serves 4-6)

- 4 tbl. butter
- 1 med. onion, minced
- 1 med. carrot, minced
- 1 stalk celery, minced
- 1 red pepper destemmed, deseeded and minced
- 2 cloves garlic, minced
- 3 tbl. flour
- 2 cups chicken broth
- 1-12 oz. bottle flat beer
- 28 oz. Half and Half cream
- 1 bay leaf
- Pinch cayenne pepper
- 1 tbl. worcestershire sauce
- 1/2 tsp. dry mustard
- 6 strips cooked bacon, diced
- 1 lb. grated sharp cheddar cheese
- Popped popcorn for garnish

In a large pot or dutch oven with a heavy bottom, melt butter and saute onion until translucent. Add carrot, red pepper, celery, and garlic and saute 2 minutes. Add flour and stir to coat veggies. When flour starts to brown (about 2 minutes), whisk in chicken stock, beer and Half and Half gradually. Turn heat to medium, add bay leaf and bring to a boil. Reduce heat and simmer 3 minutes. Remove from heat and add worcestershire sauce, cayenne, bacon, and dry mustard. Stir. Slowly add cheese, stirring until melted. Remove bay leaf and serve immediately. Top with popped popcorn. Boy, do those cheeseheads know how have to fun!!!

Homemade Mac and Cheese

The kids will never want that stuff from the blue box again. Try this out and have the kids give you a hand. I like to start with the basic recipe and just add whatever I like for that day (i.e.: chopped onions, green or red peppers, mushrooms, etc.).

- 2 cups elbow macaroni, cooked to package directions and drained
- 1 tbl. olive oil
- 2 1/2 cups milk
- 2 tbl. cornstarch
- 1/2 stick butter
- 1/2 small onion, grated
- 1/2 tsp. dry mustard
- 1/4 tsp. worcestershire sauce
- Salt and pepper to taste
- 6 oz. cheddar cheese, shredded
- 1/4 cup crushed saltine crackers or Italian bread crumbs
- Fresh parsley (optional)

Grease a two quart casserole dish with olive oil or butter. Put cooked macaroni in casserole and toss with 1 tbl. olive oil. Stir cornstarch into milk in a med. saucepan. Add butter, onion, mustard, worcestershire sauce, and salt/pepper to taste. Over medium heat stir constantly and bring to a boil. Lower heat and gradually add cheese. Continue to stir for about 2 minutes or until cheese melts. Mix with macaroni and sprinkle crackers or bread crumbs on top. Bake in preheated oven at 350 degrees until cheese is bubbly, about 10 minutes. Garnish individual servings with sprigs of fresh parsley.

Blue Cheese and Red Onion Hamburgers

There is really nothing difficult about making these, but they are a wonderful delight and a great alternative to your basic cheeseburger. I always try to use a good quality blue cheese. Buy some really good buns, a good coarse ground mustard, and your favorite dill pickle spears or slices. Now let's do lunch.

(serves 4)

2 lbs. 90% fat free ground beef
4 oz. blue cheese or gorganzola
Salt and pepper
1 loaf rustic type bread, cut into 8 slices

1 red onion, sliced
Your favorite pickles
Good coarse ground brown mustard
2 fresh tomatoes, sliced thick

Divide ground beef into 8 equal portions. Roll into balls and flatten into 1/4 inch patties. Put 1 oz. blue cheese on each of four patties leaving the pattie edges free of cheese. Place remaining patties on top and compress edges. Salt/pepper to taste. On a cleaned surface of a preheated gas barbeque grille set at medium or a charcoal grille about the same temperature, grill burgers approximately 5-7 minutes a side. Meat should no longer be pink inside. Take off grille. Slather 4 slices of bread with mustard. Top with onion slices, pickles, tomato and remaining bread slices. Serve with a cold beverage and let your hair down and relax with friends.

Evening Omelettes with Brenda

Want to have a romantic evening with hardly any fuss? You can make these up in 10-15 minutes. Add a little soft jazz, a chilled Pinot Grigio or iced tea, and a twinkle in your eye. Romance was never any easier.

- 5 large eggs (preferably fresh from the farmers market)
- 1 tbl. cream or milk
- 1 tbl. olive oil
- 1/4 red onion, chopped fine
- 1 small garlic clove, minced
- 1/2 green pepper, diced
- 3-4 oz. of your favorite cheese (I like pepper jack in this dish)
- 4-5 fresh basil leaves
- Salt and pepper
- 1 large fresh tomato, sliced

Break eggs into a small bowl. Whisk in cream/milk until thoroughly mixed. In a non-stick saute pan, heat oil and saute onions, garlic, and green pepper until onion starts to soften. Add egg mixture and start to cook over low to medium heat. Chop fresh basil and spread over eggs. When eggs begin to set, slide a rubber spatula under the mixture and around. Allow uncooked egg on top to run underneath and set. That done, run spatula again around and under to loosen mixture and help flip over. Grate or crumble cheese on one half. Flip non cheese half on top of cheese half. Let cook until cheese is melted. Divide into two servings. Add some fresh tomato slices to each plate and light the candles. Oh my!

Garlic Cheese Biscuits

I always get a big smile on my face when I go to someone's house and they serve biscuits. They just don't get the attention they used to in this fast paced society. So enlighten your guests with these melt-in-your-mouth morsels. Heavenly!!

Biscuit Flour Mix

- 2 cups all purpose flour
- 3/4 tbl. baking powder
- 1/4 heaping tsp salt
- 1/3 cup vegetable shortening
- 2/3 cup buttermilk
- 3/4 cup shredded sharp cheddar cheese
- 2 garlic cloves minced very fine
- 2 tbl. butter

Sift flour, baking powder, and salt 2-3 times in a large bowl. Cut in shortening with pastry blender or fork it in. Continue until mixture is fine crumbs.

Add buttermilk, cheddar cheese, and minced garlic to biscuit flour mix. Preheat oven to 450 degrees. Cover a cookie sheet with foil. On a lightly floured surface fold dough unto itself several times to make less sticky. Gently, ever so gently, roll dough into a 1/2 inch diameter log. With pastry cutter cut into half inch slices which you immediately transfer to the cookie sheet. Bake 8-10 minutes. While biscuits are baking, melt butter. When biscuits are golden brown, pull from oven and brush with melted butter. Serve immediately

Quiche Lorraine

At the Cafe' Deluxe we would always serve quiche as a special for Sunday morning breakfast. Quiche Lorraine was a great favorite. It is very easy to make, and you'll get some oohs and ahhs from your brunch guests. We would serve it with some fresh tomato slices on the side and garnish with a parsley sprig.

Quiche Ingredients

- Pie dough
- 2 cups whole milk
- 3 large eggs
- 1/4 tsp salt
- 1/8/ tsp white pepper
- Sprinkle of fresh nutmeg (if available)
- 1/4 lb just cooked bacon, diced
- 4 green onions, chopped fine (lower green/white parts only)
- 1 cup grated Swiss cheese

Pie Dough

- 1/2 cup chilled butter plus 3 tbl lard or shortening
- 2 cups unbleached white flour
- 1/2 tsp salt
- 5-6 tbl cold water

Work butter/lard/shortening mixture with the flour and very gently in a bowl. Rotate between hands until it becomes a crumbly flour meal. Bunch up and make a well in the center. Swirl the cold water into the well using your index finger and quickly moving from inside to gradually outside. You should have a soft ball of dough that doesn't stick to your hands. Refrigerate for 2-24 hours wrapped in plastic wrap. Press into a deep 9" pie pan. Combine milk, eggs, salt, pepper, and nutmeg. Whisk until thoroughly mixed. You now have a custard mix. Set aside. Spread bacon and green onions over bottom crust. Add grated swiss cheese. Pour custard mixture in next. Place on middle rack of a preheated oven at 375 degrees for 35-45 minutes until top is golden brown.

Mozzarella, Tomato & Basil Bruschetta

Here's a nice little appetizer that's sort of a tribute to the flag of Italy. I only make these when tomatoes are coming in ripe, out of the garden. It really makes a huge difference in flavor.

1/2 cup extra virgin olive oil
2 garlic cloves, minced
Pinch of salt
1 long loaf rustic french type bread

4 fresh ripe tomatoes
1 1/2 lbs. mozzarella cheese (20 slices/ "fresh" if available)
20 fresh basil leaves
Salt and pepper

Put olive oil, garlic, and a pinch of salt into a small sauce pan and bring to a low boil stirring occasionally. Turn off heat. Slice french bread into 20 slices. Preheat broiler. Place french bread slices on a cookie sheet. Toast under broiler until golden, maybe 30 seconds or so. Take out, turn over, and repeat. Brush olive oil mixture on top of each piece. Slice tomatoes into 20 slices. Place on top of each piece of toast. Place cheese slice on top of tomato and return under the broiler. Broil until cheese is browned, 10-15 seconds. Top each slice with a basil leaf. Salt and pepper to taste and sprinkle a little extra virgin olive oil on. Serve as an hors d' oeuvres with a nice dry red wine.

Chef's hint: if tomato and/or cheese are too large for the toast just cut down to the size you like to see.

Cheese Enchiladas

You can make cheese enchiladas with either a green sauce or a red sauce. I sometimes do both in the same baking dish. It adds a nice touch. This is a traditional simple recipe to which I never have any qualms of adding any additional ingredients. Red pepper slices, black olives, even ground sausage, use your imagination, and just have a little fun with it

(serves 4-6)

- 4 cups red chili sauce (see page 24) or store bought red enchilada sauce
- 12- 6 inch corn tortillas
- 8 oz. shredded Monterey Jack cheese
- 1 medium red onion, diced
- 1-4 oz. can diced green chilies
- 8 oz. sour cream

Preheat oven to 425 degrees. Warm up chili sauce in large skillet over medium high heat. When chili sauce is at a simmer, use a tongs and lower a tortilla in and hold until limp (about 10 seconds). This gets a little messy but the result is worth it. In a 8" x 12" x 2" casserole dish place tortilla on bottom. Add 2 tbl. cheese and 1 tbl. diced onion. Roll up and move to one end of dish seam side down. Repeat until all tortillas are filled and rolled. When you run out of room to roll in the casserole, just start placing made up tortillas on top of previously finished tortillas. Stir in diced green chilies and sour cream into remaining sauce. Pour over tortillas. Bake for 20 minutes. Sprinkle with remaining cheese and bake another 5 minutes or until cheese melts.

Very Grilled Cheese Sandwiches and Fresh Tomato Soup

Remember growing up and your mom would make grilled cheese sandwiches made with Velveeta cheese on white bread and canned tomato soup? You lived for those days. Well here is an adult version that I think you will live for as well.

Grilled Cheese Sandwiches

(serves 4)

- 8 slices rustic bread
- 12 oz. your favorite sliced cheese such as cheddar or pepper jack
- 1/2 red onion sliced in thin rings
- Remoulade sauce to spread on bread (See page 40)
- Butter

Butter 1 side of 2 slices of bread. Place in a large skillet butter side down. Cover with cheese and add onion. Spread remoulade sauce on 1 side of 2 slices of bread. Place on onion and cheese sauce side down. Butter top sides. Cook over medium heat in a large skillet until bread is toasted. Flip and toast the side. Repeat with the other 2 sandwiches.

Fresh Tomato Soup

(serves 20)

- 2 tbl. extra virgin olive oil
- 2 med. red onions, diced
- 4 cloves garlic, minced
- 10 lbs. fresh meaty tomatoes (cored and skinned)
- 8 cups chicken broth
- 2 large handfuls fresh basil (shredded)
- 1 1/2-2 cups heavy cream
- salt and fresh ground pepper

Saute onions and garlic in olive until translucent. In a large pot, add to tomatoes and chicken broth. Bring to a boil, reduce to simmer for 30 minutes. In batches blend with basil. Return to pot. Add cream to thicken as desired over low heat. Do not boil. Salt and pepper to taste.

Note: place tomatoes in boiling water to loosen skins.

The Mighty Yellow Condiment, or Do You Know the Mustard Man?

If you don't, then hop in your car, pickup truck, bicycle, tricycle, John Deere tractor, or whatever means of conveyance available, and head to Mt. Horeb, Wisconsin. Mt. Horeb is the home of the world's fabulous and famous Mustard Museum, and the Mustard Man himself, curator Barry Levenson.

The Mustard Museum began when Barry Levenson found himself awash in grief after his beloved Red Sox lost the seventh game of the 1986 World Series. He went to a all-night grocery, roamed the aisles, and heard the voice coming from the mustards: "If you collect us, they will come." He did and they have.

The Mustard Museum houses a collection of over 4400 different mustards from all over the United States and over 60 countries around the world. When it comes to collecting one of the world's oldest condiments, Barry has certainly proven that he can certainly cut the "mustard." Without further ado, here are some mustard inspired recipes with a little help from Poupon U.

Shrimp Remoulade

If you can't find creole mustard use a good coarse ground brown mustard. The remoulade sauce also works well as vegetable dip. Always make sure it is chilled thoroughly and the flavors have time to blend with each other.

(serves 6-8)

Remoulade Sauce

- 1 cup mayonnaise
- 1/2 cup brown Creole type mustard
- 4 tbl. fresh grated horseradish
- 1 tbl. paprika
- 1/2 tsp red cayenne pepper
- 6 green onions, chopped fine (white and light parts only)
- 1 rib celery, diced fine
- 2 tbl. minced fresh parsley

- 2 lb. 30-40 count shrimp (peeled and deveined)
- 1 large head iceberg lettuce, chopped or shredded
- 3 large lemons, cut into wedges

Whisk mayonnaise, mustard, horseradish, paprika, and red pepper together in a medium sized bowl. Mix in green onion, celery, and parsley. Use plastic wrap to cover and chill for 2-3 hours. Immerse shrimp in boiling water until shrimp turns pink (4-5 minutes). Drain immediately and cool down. Place shrimp in a medium sized bowl. Add enough remoulade sauce to coat evenly. Save any remaining sauce to serve on the side. Cover shrimp and chill 4-6 hours. Divide lettuce on table plates. Divide shrimp on top. Serve with lemon wedges and remaining remoulade sauce.

Green Chile and Jack Cheese Wontons with Mustard Dipping Sauce

I have a good chef friend, Greg, who came up with these wontons for a party we attended. He and I spent an hour or so frying them up and passing them out as fast as they were done. I made them later and added the mustard dipping sauce. Good job, Greg!

(makes 40 appetizers)

- peanut or corn oil
- 40 wonton skins
- 8 oz. Monterey jack cheese (cut into 40 small pieces)
- 12 green chiles (roasted, deskinned, destemmed, deseeded, and minced) or 2-4 oz. cans diced green chiles
- 1 cup sour cream
- 1/4 cup spicy brown mustard
- 2 cloves garlic, minced fine

Heat about 1 inch of oil in a heavy skillet to 350 degrees. In the meantime, place a piece of cheese just over center on a wonton skin. Add a little green chile. Wet the two side wonton edges the cheese is on and fold the remaining skin over the top. Press the top edges into the wet edges to seal. Make 6 or 8 this way. When oil is at 350, (do not go hotter or oil could burn, use a candy thermometer to check temperature) start putting wontons in skillet. Cook for about 15 seconds and flip with a slotted spoon or tongs. When golden brown, drain on paper towels. Mix sour cream, mustard and garlic thoroughly for dipping sauce. I like to make sauce ahead of time and have it well chilled. Let the party begin!!

Fresh Pretzels with Mustard Green Onion Dip

We have a good audience participation with this dish. You can have the kids help roll out and shape the pretzels. I would keep them away from the boiling water, however.

(makes 16 pretzels)

1 pkg. dry yeast
1 cup 105 degree water
2 3/4 cups white flour, sifted
3 tbl. butter (room temperature)
1 tbl. sugar

1/2 tsp. salt coarse salt
1/2 cup your favorite mustard
1/2 cup mayonnaise
1/2 cup green onions, diced small

Dissolve yeast in water. In a mixer, beat 1 1/2 cups flour, butter, sugar, and 1/2 tsp salt. Beat for 4 minutes. Add in remaining flour and knead on a floured surface. When dough is no longer sticky, place in a greased bowl and let rise until doubled. Push dough down. Roll into a log and cut into 16 equal pieces. Roll into pencil sized pieces. Take one end and loop across the middle of the pencil dough. Loop the other end over the first loop. Place on greased baking pan. Let rise until doubled. Preheat oven to 500 degrees. In a non-aluminum pan, boil 4 cups of water. Add 2 tbl. baking soda. Use a spatula to lower pretzels in. When they float, return to cookie sheet. Sprinkle with coarse salt. Bake for 10-12 minutes or until they just start to turn brown. Mix mustard, mayonnaise, and green onions. Serve with pretzels.

Easy, So Easy Rouladan

This dish originates from Germany and has a great combination of totally different flavors. I called up my butcher, John, and asked if he could cut some 1/4" strips of top round for me. He asked "Are you making Rouladan?" I asked "How did you know?" And he answered that a German lady, Irene, has him make the same cut all the time. Talk about small town culture, she and my mom, are best friends, and both immigrants from Germany, but mom never made this for us. Oh, the cuisine we missed.

- 2 lbs. top beef round, sliced into inch strips
- Coarse ground mustard
- 8 slices prosciutto 4 inches wide by 8 inches
- 12 green onions 4 inches long
- 12- 4 inch pickle slices green onion sized
- 1/4 stick of butter
- 1 1/4 cups beef broth, homemade or store bought
- Flour, salt, and pepper

Have your butcher cut 4 slices off of a top beef round into 1/4 inch strips. They should be about 12" long by 4" wide. Lay beef slices out flat and generously spread mustard over to cover. Cover each beef slice with two slices of prosciutto. You may have to overlap in the center. Cut each strip into thirds. On each third place an onion and pickle almost at the end. Take the onion and pickle end and roll up tightly. Tie with butchers twine if you have it or use toothpicks to secure it. Repeat until all are secured. Melt butter in a large skillet and brown rollups on all sides over medium heat. Add beef broth and simmer gently for 1/2 hour. Turn off heat and remove rollups to a plate. Mix thoroughly about 3 tbls. flour with a cup of cold water. Bring remaining juices in skillet to a boil. Slowly add flour mixture and stir until gravy is at desired thickness. Salt and pepper to taste. Plate up a couple rollups and pour a little gravy over. Maybe serve with some garlic smashed potatoes. Now that's Teutonic!

Mustard Glazed Baked Ham

Because Iowa is one of the leading pork producing states in the USA, we have access to an abundance of great ham. We always serve it at Thanksgiving. One of the many ways I've prepared it is the following, slathered with a good coarse ground dark mustard. I continually baste it with some sweet Red Zinfandal wine and it is truly a smash. Make sure to have enough mustard on hand for sandwiches later.

(serves 18-20)

1 14-16 lb. bone-in smoked ham
Coarse ground dark mustard
Sweet Red Zinfandel wine

Preheat oven to 325 degrees. Remove ham from all packaging including netting if encased with. Use a long carving knife to slice 1/2" deep cuts about 1" apart all across ham. Repeat at 180 degrees to create a diamond grid pattern on face of ham. Place in roasting pan fat side up. Slather with mustard. Bake 1 hour. Baste with some wine. Baste every 1/2 hour or so and add more mustard, if necessary. Bake 18-20 minutes for each pound of ham. When ham reaches an internal temperature of 160 degrees on a meat thermometer, it is ready to take out of oven. Let rest 10 minutes before carving.

Bacon and Spinach Salad with Mustard Dressing

I've always liked the combination of bacon and spinach. They compliment each other well. The mustard dressing is served warm and makes for an interesting and delightful *menage a trois* of flavors.

(serves 4)

1 lb. fresh spinach, washed and stemmed
1 lb. chopped bacon
1 tbl. dijon type mustard
2 tbl. red wine vinegar
1 tbl. honey salt and fresh ground black pepper
1 small red onion, sliced thin
2-3 hard boiled eggs, sliced

Using a heavy skillet, fry bacon over medium heat until crisp. Remove to paper towels. Save bacon drippings. Pour in a small bowl. Whisk mustard, vinegar, and honey into drippings to make the dressing. Season with salt and pepper. Toss spinach with dressing and bacon pieces. Serve a in nice salad bowl and top with sliced onions and eggs.

Honey Mustard Crusted Pork Loin with Black Raspberry Jam

Pork Loin just doesn't get any better than this. Sometimes a great dish is created out of just plain old necessity. (or I forget to pick up oranges at the store that I was going to make the sauce with.) I didn't have time to run back to the store, so it was time to wing it. I used black raspberry jam in lieu of oranges, what a treat! The blackberry flavor with pork is a true marriage made in heaven. If you have fresh or frozen Blackberries/raspberries, don't be afraid to use them instead of the jam.

(serves 4-6)

1 3-4 lb. fresh pork loin
Salt and fresh ground black pepper
Blackberry jam or blackberries to cover
4 slices prosciutto

2 oz. grated parmesan cheese
1 oz. dijon style mustard
2 oz. honey

Cut the pork loin down the center lengthwise in half. Season with salt and pepper both sides. Sear on a barbeque grille both sides 2-3 minutes a side. This adds a nice char flavor. Lay pork pieces on a cutting board or flat surface flat side up. Spread jam or berries over one side to cover. Layer prosciutto slices on top. Sprinkle parmesan over the prosciutto. In a small bowl mix mustard and honey. Place remaining pork piece on top of covered piece. Pin with toothpicks. Glaze with mustard honey mixture. In a shallow bake at 325 degrees for an additional 30-40 minutes until pork reaches an internal temperature of 165 degrees and is no longer pink or just barely inside.

Asparagus and Red Onion with Dijon Parmesan Sauce

Steaming!! That's what this recipe is all about. I prefer to steam asparagus rather than boil it. I also like to serve it "Al Dente" which means still firm and crisp. You'll like the combination of dijon mustard and parmesan as they accompany the asparagus and red onion. Lots of nice flavors here.

(Makes 4-6 sides)

1 lb. fresh asparagus (thin stalks preferred)
1/2 red onion, halved and sliced thin
6 slices smoked bacon, diced and fried crisp
1/2 cup extra virgin olive oil
4 tbl. fresh lemon juice
1 tbl. dijon mustard
3 tbl. fresh grated parmesan cheese
Salt and fresh ground black pepper to taste

Trim asparagus. Using a steamer or a metal colander over a pot of boiling water, steam asparagus and onion until just tender. (10-14 minutes, depending on the thickness of the asparagus). Put in serving container along with the bacon. While steaming process is going on, combine remaining ingredients and blend in food processor or blender. Warm in a small pan and pour over asparagus mixture.

Sauteed Turkey Breast with Basil and Creole Mustard Cream

I combined a couple of very different tastes to bring this together. I really like basil and the way it compliments a lot of different foods. Toss in a little creole mustard and you're having a party. A little parmesan cheese thrown in at the end and just melted adds another great dimension if you want just a little more zip.

(serves 6-8)

2 1/2 lbs. fresh boneless turkey breast
2 tbl. butter
1/2 green pepper, sliced thin
1/2 red onion, sliced thin
1/2 cup heavy cream
1 tsp. cajun seasoning
fresh ground black pepper
1 tbl. grated parmesan cheese
6-8 fresh leaves basil
8 oz. fettucine noodles, cooked to package directions and drained

Slice turkey breast diagonally into 1/4 strips. Melt butter in a heavy bottomed skillet. Saute turkey for 2 minutes on each side or until cooked thoroughly. Remove from skillet. Saute green pepper and onion until soft. Remove skillet from heat and whisk in mustard. Return to low to medium heat and whisk in heavy cream. Add cajun seasoning, pepper, and parmesan cheese. Put turkey slices back in, chop and add basil, and heat 1-2 minutes. Serve up noodles on plates, spoon turkey on top and ladle sauce over.

Chicken with Mango Mustard Salsa

We are talking salsa here. I had some salsa left over the last time I made it. I came home from work. Brenda was just eating it out of the bowl and raving about it. Definitely a fun chicken dish, and take it from Brenda, the salsa stands on it's own.

(serves 3-4)

1-3 1/2 to 4 lb. chicken, cut up into 8 pieces
8 oz. coarse ground brown mustard
5 medium ripe tomatoes, diced
1 large red onion, diced
1 large green pepper diced
5 cloves garlic, minced

5 jalepenos destemmed, deseeded, and minced
2 ripe mangos peeled, cored, and diced
Salt and fresh ground black pepper to taste
Fresh iceberg lettuce

Preheat oven to 350 degrees. Place chicken skin side up in a greased shallow 9 x 14 baking. Mix remaining ingredients in a large bowl. Puree 1/2 of the mixture in a food processor. Pour over chicken and put in oven. Bake for 50-60 minutes or until when the thickest chicken pieces are pierced with a knife, the juices run clear. Put remaining salsa in refrigerator and chill while chicken is baking. When chicken is ready to serve, plate up, lay down some lettuce, and ladle some chilled salsa on. Eat a little chicken, fork down a little mango salsa, and just enjoy the day.

Salad Daze

And the question of the day is two part: In what city and country was Caesar salad invented and what is Oscar Tshirky famous for? If you said Tijuana, Mexico and Waldorf salad, you probably should be writing your own darn cookbook. Welcome to the salad bowl, ladies and gentlemen! It can be the main event or a sensational sideshow. Every once in a while when I was growing up, my mom would make salad which consisted of chopped iceberg lettuce and French/Western dressing. The restaurant I worked at and others we ate at pushed it to the limit by adding a choice of Thousand Island or Bleu Cheese dressing. HOLY CLAM DIP!!!

While in college, I campaigned for a governor's race in La Crosse, WI, for a couple of days. A doctor and his wife gave me a place to stay and fed me supper. And can you believe the doctor's wife had taken iceberg lettuce and mixed in romaine lettuce with fresh sliced mushrooms and red onions. She then tossed it with red wine vinegar and extra virgin olive oil. EUREKA!!! CULINARY BREAKTHROUGH!!!

We've come out of the Dark Ages, baby. So take a walk on the wild side. Go crazy. Experiment. Or what the heck, just use leftovers. Your salad may live on into infamy. You see, Caesar Cardini did just that 80 years ago, in Tijuana, Mexico.

Hail to Ceasar Salad

My wife, Brenda, could live on salad alone. Here is one of her favorites. If you have concerns of using raw egg because of salmonella risk, use a pasteurized or a coddled egg. As always, try to find the freshest ingredients, especially the lettuce.

(serves 4)

1 peeled garlic clove	2 tbl. fresh squeezed lemon juice
3/4 tsp. salt	1 tbl. red wine vinegar
1/4 tsp. fresh ground black pepper	1 tsp. Worcestershire sauce
1 tbl. Dijon mustard	6 anchovy fillets, chopped
1 large fresh egg	1 large head romaine lettuce
1/4 cup extra virgin olive oil	1/4 loaf rustic french bread (about 6 inches)

In a large serving bowl, add salt and pepper. Mash garlic clove in salt and wipe around bowl. Stir mustard in. Whisk egg into mixture. Stir in olive oil. Slowly stir in lemon and red wine vinegar. Add Worcestershire and anchovies and mix. Wash lettuce and cut off stem. Chop into large bite sized pieces and toss with dressing. Cube bread into 3/8 inch cubes. Heat about 2 tbl. olive in large skillet to medium/medium-high heat. Add bread cubes and saute until golden (about 3-4 minutes). Drain on paper towels, then salt and pepper to taste. Garnish salad with bread cubes (croutons) and serve immediately. Pass around fresh grated parmesan cheese.

Chef's note: Add 1 egg to boiling water for exactly 1 minute. Take out, break shell, and whisk for coddled egg.

Beef and Horseradish Salad

Every year we get a few of the boys together and dig horseradish. This process requires cleaning the horseradish in an old agitator washing machine. We then have to peel it all. We use a hand crank meat grinder to process it to a coarse grated condiment. The fumes created will bring tears to your eyes in a couple of minutes. So you grind until you absolutely can't stand it anymore. Then you get up, grab a beer, and someone else takes your place. Repeat the process until done. Gee, do we know how to have fun? Talk about seeing a bunch of grown men cry!

(serves 4)

1 1/2-2 lbs. New York Strip or sirloin steak 1" thick

4 oz. teriyaki sauce

Cajun seasoning

1/2 red onion, sliced thin

Enough salad greens of your choice to heap 4 salad plates

Dressing

1 cup heavy cream

1-2 tbl. horseradish

Beat cream until thick. Add horseradish.

Marinate steak for 2 hours with teriyaki sauce. Preheat BBQ grille. Place steak on grille, add cajun seasoning, and cook, turning once, about 4 minutes a side for medium rare. Pull off grille, cover with foil and chill for 2 hours in refrigerator. Slice steak on the diagonal into 1/4 inch strips. You should have 5 or 6 strips per salad. Heap greens on 4 plates. Spread red onions over each plate. Divide steak into 4 equal portions. Start in the center of each salad and lay a steak strip from top to bottom. Continue around the salad forming a draped finger pattern. Serve with dressing on the side. Oh Yeah!!

South of the Winneshiek County Border Salad with Fresh Salsa Dressing

Have fun with different ingredients for a change. I was at work thinking of what I could make for Brenda for supper. With her love for salads, I wanted to create something a little special, but also with a different twist. If you don't have time to make a salsa, don't be afraid to buy some commercially made.

(serves 4)

Salad

1 lb. boneless skinless chicken breast

Cajun seasoning

8 oz. red or black grapes, seedless

8 oz. grape tomatoes

1/2 red onion, sliced thin

1 head romaine lettuce

1 head Boston leaf lettuce

2 ripe avocados

Fresh Salsa

3 fresh tomatoes, diced

1/2 red onion, diced

1 green pepper, cored and diced

3 garlic cloves, minced

3 jalapenos, destemmed, deseeded, and minced

2 limes

Salt and fresh ground black pepper

Preheat BBQ grille. Wash and pat dry chicken. Season with Cajun seasoning. Grille chicken, turning on both sides until no longer pink inside (about 10 minutes).

Mix tomato, onion, green pepper and jalapenos in a large bowl. Add the juice from the two limes. Salt and pepper to taste and chill for 1-2 hours.

Cut bottoms off lettuce heads. Wash lettuces and pat dry. Mix and arrange on four table plates. Spread equal amounts of grapes, tomatoes, and onion on top. Slice chicken diagonally and arrange on top of salads. Add fresh salsa to each. Peel and slice avocados. Place on top and serve right away.

Watercress Rehearsal Salad

I made this salad for a rehearsal dinner for Shanon and Kim. We sat 50 people down in our home and served up a five course meal. Eric and I went out early in the day and collected wild leeks and picked fresh watercress. Here is what we threw together.

(serves 4)

Salad
- 1 1/2 lbs. fresh watercress
- 12 wild leeks or small green onions, trimmed
- 36 red seedless grapes
- 2 large tomatoes, cored, halved, and sliced
- Grated Asiago cheese

Dressing
- 1/2 cup extra virgin olive oil
- 4 tbl. fresh lemon juice or red wine vinegar
- Salt to taste

Wash watercress and discard any large stems. Make a bed of watercress on each of 4 salad plates. Divide salad into thirds by laying 3 leeks/onions on top. Place 3 grapes on each section. Lay a tomato slice on each third and sprinkle with asiago cheese. Whisk dressing ingredients together and add to each salad. Serve immediately.

Spinach and Feta Cheese with Spicy Andouille Sauce

Every year we have a fund-raiser called "The Crystal Ball" for our local hospital. They auction off numerous items, and last year, one of them was me. I made up a 5 course menu for three different cuisines. I gave a choice of 3 items in each cuisine for each course. Dinner for 10 was served and here is their salad selection. I hope you enjoy it as much as they did.

(serves 4)

Salad
- 1 lb. fresh spinach, washed, drained and stems removed
- 1/2 red onion, sliced into thin wedges
- 1 cup feta cheese, crumbled
- Salt and fresh ground black pepper to taste

Sauce
- 3/4 cup extra virgin olive oil
- 6 oz. andouille or precooked hot italian sausage, diced
- 2-3 cloves garlic, minced
- 3 tbl. red wine vinegar

Toss spinach, onion, and feta cheese. Heat sauce ingredients in a small pot for 3-4 minutes. Mix spinach, onion and feta cheese. Add sauce to salad mixture. Serve while warm on 4 plates. Pass the salt and pepper and let everyone season their own. Enjoy!!

Morgan's Fresh Out of the Garden Summertime Pasta

Brenda's son Shanon, his girlfriend Morgan, and our grandson Kamran live just up the road from us, so we get together a lot. And, of course, they have all had to put up with me while writing this book. When Morgan asked me if I'd like to try a salad of hers for the book, I said, "Great." And it is great. I hope you enjoy it as much as we have.

(serves 8)

- 8 oz. angel hair pasta
- 2 cups fresh asparagus, cut in 1 inch pieces
- 2 cups fresh green beans, cut in 1 inch pieces
- 1/2 med. red onion, chopped
- 1 red pepper, chopped
- 1 cucumber, sliced
- 1 cup black olives
- 3 tbl. extra virgin olive oil
- 3 tbl. fresh lemon juice
- 2 tsp. lemon rind
- 1 tsp. salt
- 1/2 tsp. fresh ground black pepper

Cook pasta according to package directions. Add asparagus and beans the last 3 minutes of cooking time. Drain and cool. Add onion, pepper, cucumber, and olives. Toss. Together, mix olive oil, lemon juice, lemon rind, and salt and pepper to taste. Pour over salad and toss again. Chill for 1-2 hours. Bon appetite.

Melon and Fruit Salad

Having brunch? Want something cool and refreshing to serve your guests? This is a fun dish that you can have the youngsters give you a hand with. I like to make it a couple of hours ahead of time and make sure it gets well chilled in the refrigerator.

(16-20 servings)

- 1 small seedless watermelon
- 1 honeydew melon
- 1 cantaloupe melon
- 1/2 lb. red grapes, seedless
- 1/2 lb. green grapes, seedless
- 1 lb. fresh ripe strawberries, sliced or quartered
- 5 kiwi fruit, peeled and sliced
- 1 lemon
- 1 lime
- 1 orange
- Sugar (optional)

Use a melon baller and scoop out meat of the three melons and place in large bowl. Add grapes, strawberries, and kiwi. Squeeze out all of the juice of the lemon, lime, and orange into a small bowl. Stir thoroughly and taste. Add sugar to taste if you like. Pour over fruit salad and toss gently. Refrigerate at least a couple of hours to get the salad well chilled.

Chef's hint: If you don't have a juicer, just twist a fork in the lemon, lime and orange to help get all the juice out.

Pasta Salad with Homemade Green Goddess Dressing

Do try this at home. When you are making some other dish, like Mac's Twisted Lamb Casserole (page 123), just make extra pasta. It will stay fresh in a tight lidded container for two or three days. Macaroni shells work fine as well. The green goddess dressing really adds a great dimension.

Pasta Salad

- 8 oz. farafelle noodles, cooked according to package directions, drained and cooled
- 20 cherry tomatoes, halved
- 1 medium red onion, chopped
- 1 green pepper, diced
- 1- 6 oz. can medium black olives, drained
- 8 oz. medium cheddar cheese, diced

Combine all above ingredients and chill for an hour.

Green Goddess Dressing

- 2 cups mayonnaise
- 6 whole anchovy fillets
- 2 whole scallions
- 1/4 cup chopped fresh parsley
- 1/4 cup chopped fresh chives
- 2 tsp. fresh tarragon
- 2 tbl. red wine vinegar
- 1 tsp. salt
- Fresh ground pepper (5-7 turns)

Place all dressing ingredients in food processor and blend until smooth Add dressing to chilled salad. Talk about living right.

Brenda's Bountiful Brunch Salad

We never have a problem getting this salad eaten up. We use lots of ingredients that complement each other, adding layer upon layer. It's just great fun. I try to make different symmetrical designs, depending on which ingredient I am using.

(serves 8-12)

- 1 head romaine lettuce, trimmed and chopped
- 1 head Boston lettuce, trimmed and chopped
- 1/2 large red onion, cut into thin rings
- 6 oz. can medium sized black olives, drained
- 6 oz. jar pimiento stuffed green olives
- 2 large red peppers, cored and sliced into rings
- 6 oz. red or black grapes, seedless
- 2-3 fresh tomatoes, cored and sliced into thin wedges
- 4 oz. feta or other goat cheese

In a large salad bowl, mix up the lettuce. Layer onion rings over the top. Spread black and green olives on onions, then layer red pepper rings over top. Add grapes. Starting at the outside edge of bowl, place tomato wedges side by side around the bowl until you have made a complete circle. Repeat on inside of circle until salad is covered. Sprinkle with feta cheese and pass around your favorite salad dressings.

Heavenly Coleslaw

This is a favorite of mine, especially if we are making a spicy item on the grill. Make sure it is well chilled. The crisp coolness helps offset the spiciness. As always, look for cabbage that appears fresh and the leaves look crisp. Limpy cabbage will not stand up for this salad. Enjoy!

(serves 12)

- 1 medium green cabbage, cored and shredded
- 1 medium red cabbage, cored and shredded
- 3 carrots, peeled and grated
- 4 sets green onions, diced small (white and light green parts only)

- 8 tbl. extra virgin olive oil
- 6 tbl. red wine vinegar
- 6 tbl. fresh lemon juice
- 4 tbl. white sugar
- 1 tsp. dry mustard
- 2 tsp. caraway seed

Combine cabbage, carrots, and green onions. Toss. In a food processor or blender, combine the remaining ingredients and blend well. Pour over cabbage mixture and toss well. Refrigerate 2-4 hours. Toss again before serving. Yum!!

Waldorf Salad

I just couldn't help myself. Here is our version of this classic salad. I figured Oscar should have his fair share of recognition. This is a nice combination of different ingredients and presents well.

(serves 6-8)

- 2 tart and crisp apples (Granny Smith, Cortland, etc.)
- 1 celery stalk, chopped
- 6 oz. chopped walnuts
- 1 cup grapes
- 1 cup broccoli florets
- 1 cup mayonnaise
- Juice of 1 lemon
- Salad greens

Wash apples and remove stem. Cut in half. Slice into 1/4 inch slices, then cube slices. In a medium mixing bowl, add apples, celery, walnuts, grapes and broccoli. Mix well with mayonnaise and lemon juice. Refrigerate for 2 hours or overnight. When ready to serve, place salad greens on salad plates and add a helping of cooled salad. This is good stuff.

Chef's note: We added the grapes and broccoli to the original recipe. It just adds another dimension. Feel free to add your own extra ingredients. After all, we're just making salad!!

My Favorite Irish Joke

Mrs. Pete Monaghan came into the newsroom to pay for her husband's obiturary. She was told by the kindly newsman that it was a dollar a word and he remembered Pete and wasn't it too bad about him passing away.

She thanked him for his kind words and bemoaned the fact that she only had two dollars. But she wrote out the obituary, "Pete died."

The newsman said he thought old Pete deserved more and he'd give her three more words at no charge.

Mrs. Pete Monaghan thanked him and rewrote the obituary: "Pete died. Boat for sale"

Mushroom Mania

The mighty morel! What a culinary pleasure! Although morels are found throughout the United States, the Midwest is a hot bed for these delectable delights. Shrooming, the art of picking morels, is a stealth sport. Shroomers are passionate about their picking and the secret spots where they find morels. This is a sport where grown men and women are crawling around on their hands and knees through the brambles and the bushes in the woods for days.

"5 Top Lies by Shroomers"

5. They are not out yet.

4. I've trained my dog to sniff them out.

3. I'm just out here picking spring flowers.

2. I found them 5 miles from here.

1. Sure, I have permission to hunt here.

Hunting morels is one of my favorite pastimes. They are wily and elusive, but there is nothing more exciting than looking down at your feet and seeing one, then two, no three. HOLY KUMQUAT!!! IT'S THE MOTHERLODE!!! Recipes for these and other mushrooms are on the agenda for this chapter.

Did you hear the one about the two mushrooms who walked into a bar and ordered a of couple beers? The bartender refused to serve them and asked them to leave. A bar patron asks, "Why did you did that? They looked like a couple of 'fungis'."

Morel and Green Chile Soup

When we had "McCaffrey's Supper Club," we always had two or three soups on. Here is a version of our signature soup. If morels are out of season, just substitute with what is available, even sliced button mushrooms will work. The soup won't be quite the same, but it will still be delicious. We can our morels and the juice left from parboiling them before the canning process. You can substitute chicken broth here with very acceptable results.

(12-16 servings)

Morel Broth

- 3 qts. chicken broth
- 1 qt. canned morel juice OR 1 qt .chicken broth
- 1 pint canned morels OR 4 oz. dried morels soaked in warm water, 30 minutes
- 3-4 green chiles (roasted, skinned, destemmed, and deseeded) OR 1-4 oz. can diced green chiles
- 1 small red onion, diced
- 3 cloves garlic, minced
- Salt and fresh ground black pepper to taste

Roux

2 1/4 sticks butter   2 cups flour

Combine all 'MOREL BROTH' ingredients in large pot and bring to a boil. Reduce to a simmer and cover. Melt butter in 2-3 gallon heavy bottom pot over low heat. Add flour and stir constantly for 12 minutes, pulling off heat occasionally. Do not let burn. If you see black flecks you will have to start over. Turn off heat. This is your ROUX. Pour broth into roux pot and stir. Turn heat back on low/medium heat and cook until soup thickens (1-3 minutes). Get ready for heaven!!

Portabella Pizzettes

I brought some homemade pizzas down to our favorite watering hole, "Your Place," to share with the gang. We got talking about pizza and Lane asked me if I had ever made pizza using portabella caps as a base. I hadn't, but of course I had to try it. These are great as appetizers or even a light supper.

(8 appetizers or first course starters)

8 large portabella caps
Extra virgin olive oil
15 oz. Basic Red Sauce (page 102)
1 lb. hot bulk Italian sausage, crumbled, fried, and drained

1/2 red onion, diced
1 green pepper, diced
1 lb. mozzarella cheese, grated

Preheat oven to 400 degrees. Brush off mushroom caps. Remove stems, if any. Gently, ever so gently, scrape out gills on the underside of the caps. Brush top side of caps with olive oil. Arrange mushrooms, cap side down, on a cookie sheet. Spoon red sauce into each cap like you would on a pizza crust. Top with Italian sausage, onion, and green pepper. Sprinkle mozzarella cheese over the top. Place cookie sheet on the middle rack of preheated oven and bake 7-8 minutes. Keep an eye on these as the mushrooms can be a little fragile if you overcook them. Since no two ovens seem to cook the same, you might want to experiment with one before you make the entire batch. Also, don't limit yourself to the ingredients I have included. Anything you like on pizza will go well here.

Stuffed Mushrooms

Your guests will keep coming back for more. We serve these tasty appetizers for many different types of gatherings and they are always a hit. I usually try to get the larger button mushrooms from my produce man. They hold more of the stuffing. If you can't keep a mushroom from falling over, just use a knife and cut a flat bottom on it.

(makes 24 appetizers)

- 24 large button mushrooms
- 1 lb. ground pork sausage, crumbled, precooked, and drained
- 2- 8 oz. pkgs cream cheese
- 1/2 cup Italian bread crumbs
- 1/2 red onion, diced fine
- 2 garlic cloves, minced
- 1/4 cup chopped fine fresh parsley
- 1 1/4 lb stick butter
- Fresh grated parmesan cheese

Preheat oven to 350 degrees. Brush clean the mushrooms. Remove stems from mushroom caps and chop fine. Thoroughly mix chopped stems with cooked pork sausage, cream cheese, red onion, garlic, and parsley until cream cheese is spread consistently throughout the mixture.

Melt butter. Place mushroom caps, destemmed side down, on a cookie sheet. Brush with melted butter and turn over. Roll a mixture of stuffing mix in your hand about the size of a golf ball. Gently press into a mushroom cap. Repeat until all caps are filled. Sprinkle with fresh parmesan or asiago cheese. Bake in preheated oven 20-25 minutes. Serve immediately.

Mushrooms in White Wine

Simmer, simply simmer. Also, simply scrumptious. If I were a mushroom, here is where I would want to make my grand culinary debut. Of course, it would also be my exit, but what a way to go.

(appetizers for 4)

1/2 lb. baby portebella mushrooms
1/2 lb. white button mushrooms
1 1/2 sticks butter
4 large cloves, minced

Salt and fresh ground black pepper
2 cups white Chablis wine
1/4 cup chopped parsley
1 small loaf rustic bread, sliced thick

Clean mushrooms with a damp cloth. You want to have bite sized pieces here, so if mushrooms are large, cut in half or quarter them. Melt butter in a large heavy bottomed skillet. Add mushrooms and garlic. Salt and pepper to taste. Saute over low/medium heat until mushrooms begin to lose their water (about 5-7 minutes). Add more butter if mushrooms begin to absorb too much. Add white wine and bring to a simmer. Cover the skillet with a lid just off center so some moisture can escape. Simmer over low heat for 25-30 minutes or until moisture is reduced to half. Sprinkle parsley over and stir. Serve up and have bread ready for sopping up the fragrant juices. Out of this world!!!

Mushroom and Red Onion Stroganoff

When you cater events such as we do, it's inevitable that you end up with extra ingredients. I had a lot of fresh button mushrooms on hand and made up this no fuss recipe. The Italian sausage really brings it together.

(serves 8-12)

16 oz. medium egg noodles
1 1/2 lb. hot ground Italian sausage
1 lb. white button mushrooms, sliced

1 medium red onion, diced
3 cloves garlic, minced
2-16 oz. containers sour cream

Boil egg noodles according to package directions. Drain and keep warm. In a large skillet, brown Italian sausage and drain. Place in a large pot and add mushrooms, onions, and garlic. Cook over medium heat until mushrooms start to lose their water (about 5 minutes). Add sour cream and noodles and heat through. Serve immediately.

Sauteed Mushroom Pizza

A true mushroom lovers delight. This recipe calls for sliced fresh button mushrooms, but you can really use anything you like. Morels, Chantrelles or Oyster mushrooms would be great for this recipe. I didn't use a red sauce here, although if you prefer, go for it. Be creative, add whatever you like with mushrooms. Late night delivery, anyone?

(serves 2-3)

Basic pizza dough
  (see Pizza Time, page 104)
Corn meal
1/2 lb. fresh button mushrooms, sliced
2 tbl. extra virgin olive oil
1 small white onion, diced
2 garlic cloves, minced
Salt
Fresh ground black pepper
8-10 oz. mozzarella cheese
2 oz. parmesan cheese
Coarse red pepper flakes (if desired)

Make pizza dough. This recipe has enough ingredients for one 12 inch pizza. Preheat oven to 450-475 degrees. In the bottom of a large skillet, heat olive oil. Add mushrooms and saute for 2 minutes. Add onion and garlic and season with salt and pepper to your taste. Sprinkle a little corn meal on the bottom of a 12" pizza pan. Roll out pizza dough and place in pan. Spread mushroom mixture over the top of the dough. Cover with mozzarella cheese and sprinkle parmesan cheese all over. Place in preheated oven on middle shelf and bake 18-20 minutes, or until crust is toasted on the bottom and cheese is golden brown on top.

Chicken Marsala

My, my, my!!! Who said 20 minute meals can't be gourmet? Don't pass this one up. It is simplicity at it's best. You can awe your crowd with very little effort. Your culinary prowess will be lauded from coast to coast. Seriously, this is really enjoyable. A nice dry red wine (Cabernet Sauvignon, Merlot, Shiraz, etc.) accompanies this well.

(serves 4)

- 2 whole boneless chicken breasts, halved
- 3/4 cup all purpose white flour
- Salt and fresh ground black pepper to taste
- 1 tbl. olive oil
- 2 tbl. butter
- 1 cup fresh sliced button mushrooms (or whatever you prefer)
- 1 cup marsala wine
- 1 clove garlic, minced
- 1 tbl. fresh lemon juice

Place chicken breasts one at a time in a gallon food storage bag and pound with a meat hammer until breasts are 1/4 inch thick. Season flour with salt and pepper. Dredge chicken in flour and shake off any extra. In a large heavy skillet, heat olive oil and 1 tbl. butter to medium, medium/ high. Brown chicken for about three minutes a side or until golden brown and cooked through. Set aside and keep warm. Add remaining butter to pan and saute mushrooms until they start to turn brown (about 7-8 minutes). Add Marsala, garlic, and lemon juice and reduce to about 3/4 cup of liquid (about 5 minutes). Serve over chicken with your favorite pasta.

Mushroom and Scallion Omelet

In the mood to brew a fresh pot of coffee, squeeze some fresh orange juice, slice up some fresh melon and berries, and quickly make breakfast in bed for your significant other? Here is your chance to be the darling of the day. Boursin cheese is available in the specialty cheese section at your local grocery. We can get it in Decorah, population 8,000. If you can't, just substitute a cheese you like with eggs. I like to serve a good rye toast and some sliced tomatoes with this. Who knows what this might lead to?

(serves 2)

5 large eggs (preferably farm fresh)
Fresh milk
1/4 of a stick of butter
1 large scallion, minced
2 oz. your favorite fresh mushrooms, sliced thin
1/2 red pepper, halved and cut into thin 2 inch strips
2-3 oz. boursin cheese, crumbled or sliced thin

Crack open eggs in a small mixing bowl. Whisk with a little milk until smooth. Set aside. Melt butter in a saute pan over low/med heat. Add scallions, mushrooms, and red pepper and saute until mushrooms begin to lose their water. Add eggs. When bottom starts to set, use a rubber spatula around the edges to lift egg mixture. Tilt skillet and let eggs run from top to underneath. Repeat until omelet begins to set. Add boursin cheese to one side. Flip other side over on top and let cheese melt (about 1-2 minutes). Oh Yeah !!!

Sauteed Morels with Garlic

Among morel aficionados there is always a great debate as to the best preparation technique. You can roll them in flour, dip them in egg, and roll again in crushed cracker crumbs, or make a beer batter and deep fat fry. At our house, we end up doing a little of each. Brenda's favorite is the following recipe.

(makes about 4 appetizers)

1 lb. fresh morel mushrooms, cleaned
1 clove garlic, minced

Butter
Salt and fresh ground black pepper to taste

Slice mushrooms in half. If mushrooms are large, quarter them. In a large saute pan, melt butter and add mushrooms and garlic. Salt and pepper to taste. Saute 3-4 minutes. When morels start to brown a little, pull off and place on paper towels. Pat dry with another paper towel. Serve them up and you will be raving.

Chef's note: To clean morels, rinse under cold water and cut out any brown or moldy parts. Place in cold salt water and chill at least 2 hours. Drain and re-rinse. Pat dry. This will eliminate any insects nesting in the mushrooms.

Mushroom Turkey Kabobs and Darlene's Golden Rice

Scrumptious just comes to mind. You can have a gathering of friends and a number of individual types of food cut up, then everyone can put together their own kabobs. I really like to use these marinated mushrooms which really enhance any kabob you may make.

(serves 6-8)

Mushroom Kabobs

- 2 lbs. button mushrooms
- 2 lbs. turkey breast, cut into bite sized pieces
- 4 tbl. Worcestershire sauce
- 6 tbl. balsamic vinegar
- 1 cup extra virgin olive oil
- 3 tbl. minced fresh chives
- 2 garlic cloves, minced
- 1 tbl. sesame seed oil
- 1 cup orange juice
- 2 large onions, cut into 1/8's
- 3 large peppers, cut into 1" X 1" pieces
- 1/2 lb. cherry tomatoes

Mix Worcestershire, balsamic vinegar, olive oil, chives, garlic, sesame seed oil and orange juice to make marinade. If mushrooms are large, slice in half. In a large bowl, combine mushrooms, turkey, and marinade. Cover and chill 2-3 hours. Preheat BBQ grille. Have 12 metal or pre-soaked wood skewers on hand. Thread with a mushroom, a turkey piece, an onion piece, green pepper and tomato. Repeat. Grille, turning until turkey is cooked. Serve with Darlene's rice. Now that's nice!!

Darlene's Rice

- 3 cups chicken broth
- 1-1/2 cups rice
- 1/2 tsp. curry powder
- 1/2 tsp. turmeric
- 1-1/2 tbl. soy sauce
- 1/2 cup golden raisins (optional)

Mix rice with curry powder, turmeric, and soy sauce (raisins optional). In a dutch oven or large heavy duty pot, add broth and rice mixture. Bring to a boil and cover with a tight fitting lid. Simmer for 20 minutes.

Flim Flamming at the Farmer's Market

HOE! HOE! HOE! It's like Christmas in July. Just when you think you have opened your last present, Dad pulls out the red Radio Flyer wagon from behind the couch. (I have visions of sugar snap peas dancing in my head). At the farmers market, a person can walk right up and look straight into the eye of a red potato and say, "I'm going to boil you, baby, and slather you with butter." Carrots are screaming "Julienne me!!! Julienne me!!!" A hot tomato and cool cucumber looking for a good time, a fresh garlic and a couple of naked onions will make an olive oil orgy on a bed of lettuce that will make you think you have died and gone to heaven.

Live a little. Take a fruit loop around the strawberries, cherries, blueberries, apples, peaches, and plums. Hey, salivate with the sweet corn! And never underestimate the importance of being a kohlrabi. Even brussel sprouts know how to have a good time. (Remember that slathered butter thing).

Seriously, it's always been a special treat for me to attend a farmers market and be surrounded by all of the fresh produce, flowers, baked goods, eggs, herbs, and nowadays, even organic meats and cheeses. The smells are outstanding and the camaraderie can't be beat. So high-tail it down to your local market and let the slathering begin.

Kohlrabi and Sugar Snap Pea Stir Fry

I've never met a kohlrabi I didn't like. If you've never had it, you are in for a treat. I've been finding it year 'round in grocery stores besides the Farmer's Market. Peel them like an apple, slice into wedges and add a touch of salt to each wedge. That's a treat just in itself. Throw it in a stir fry such as this and you'll wonder where it's been all your life.

(4 servings)

2 cups rice	2 garlic cloves, minced
3 tbl. corn oil	1 red pepper, cored, seeded and diced
4 baseball sized kohlarbi	1 cup fresh or frozen sweet corn kernels
1/2 lb. sugar snap peas	3/4 cup teriyaki sauce
1 small red onion, diced	3/4 cup water

Place rice in a medium bowl. Rinse under cold water, stirring gently. Drain and repeat 3-4 times until water is no longer milky. This takes out a lot of the starch that makes rice sticky. Place in pot with heavy bottom and add 4 cups water. Bring to a boil. Cover with a tight lid and cook an additional 20 minutes. Turn off heat. Put 3 tbl. oil in heavy bottom skillet and bring to med-hot heat. Add all veggies and stir fry 4-5 minutes. Keeping heat on, add teriyaki and water and bring to a boil stirring once in while. Sprinkle in some corn starch, stir and let thicken. If you want it thicker just add some more cornstarch. Serve up rice and ladle stir fry over.

Roasted Garlic and Chive Smashed Potatoes

My dad, Leonard, was a great gardener. He participated in the local Farmer's Market for years. I loved to go and spend time with him in the garden. Inevitably, he would pull me aside and grinning his wonderful Irish smile, he'd hand me a fresh raw clove of garlic. What a rush! Try some with Yukon Gold potatoes and chives. Leonard would have given a thumbs up on this one.

5 lbs. yukon gold potatoes, unpeeled
1 head garlic cloves
2 tbl. olive oil
4 tbl. fresh snipped chives
1/4 lb. butter
1-2 cups buttermilk
Salt and fresh ground black pepper

Preheat oven to 375 degrees. Wash potatoes. Cover potatoes in a large pot with water and bring to a boil. Lower to simmer and cook until just tender. You should be able to put a knife through the thickest potato. While potatoes are simmering, cut off the top of the garlic head. In a small bowl put 1 tbl. olive oil and a sprinkle of salt. Rub top of garlic head in mixture. Place garlic on some foil, and pour remaining oil over. Encapsule garlic in foil and bake 20 - 30 minutes. Garlic cloves need to be soft like butter. Drain potatoes. Add butter. Squeeze garlic cloves out of husks and add. Add chives. With a hand potato masher, start mashing potato mixture. Add buttermilk a little at a time, until you achieve the consistency you desire. Add salt and pepper to taste as you are mashing.

Steamed Prosciutto Asparagus

Here is a little different wrap. The asparagus and prosciutto each have unique flavors, but they really compliment each other. I like to serve asparagus on the Al Dente side. (a little crispy) If you steam it too long it will get mushy, so keep your eye on it.

(makes 6 sides)

1 lb. fresh asparagus (the smaller in circumference, the better)
6 thin slices prosciutto
6 lemon wedges
Melted butter (optional)
Salt and fresh ground black pepper to taste

Bring a pot of water to boil. Cut thick ends off the asparagus. Divide asparagus into 6 equal portions. Wrap prosciutto around each asparagus portion and pin with a toothpick. Using a steam basket or a metal colander, steam wraps until asparagus is just tender, about 8-12 minutes. It all depends on the size of the asparagus. Serve with lemon wedges on the side and melted butter if desired. Add salt and pepper to taste.

Baked Acorn Squash

Another of Brenda's favorites. Readily available in the fall at your Farmer's Market and local grocery stores, it's nutritious besides being yummy. I usually figure a 1/2 of a squash per person. Real maple syrup is a great accompaniment also.

(serves 4)

2 acorn squash
Butter

Salt and fresh ground black pepper
Maple syrup or brown sugar (if you like it really sweet)

Preheat oven to 400 degrees. Wash squash and destem. Cut in half from top to bottom. Take out seeds and fiber. Place face down on a cookie sheet and bake for 25 minutes. Take out of oven and turn face sides up. Season with butter, salt and pepper. That is how I like to prepare this dish. However to satisfy those with a sweet tooth, add some maple syrup or brown sugar to your liking at this point. Pop back into the oven and bake another 30 minutes or so. This is some hearty fare.

Tuna Stuffed Tomatoes

What a great summer-time lunch. We would serve this at the Cafe Deluxe and we never were able to make enough it seemed. Have some iced tea or chilled Chardonnay on hand and just enjoy the day.

(serves 4)

4 large fresh ripe tomatoes
Fresh lettuce greens
3 cans chunk white tuna, drained
1/2 red onion, diced
12-16 dill pickle slices, diced

1/2-3/4 cup mayonnaise (depends on how creamy you like your tuna salad)
Salt and fresh ground black pepper
8 red radish slices

Core out tomato stems. Slice tomatoes into quarters but not quite all the way through. Put lettuce greens on a salad plate and gently top with a sliced tomato. Repeat for four servings. Mix tuna, onion, pickles, and mayonnaise well. Salt and pepper to taste. If you have one, use a large ice cream scoop and dish up tuna unto tomatoes. Garnish with two radish slices per. Yummy!!!

Grilled Zuchini Creole

The first year we cooked for Decorah's "Live On Winnebago" festival, lots of folks asked if we had anything vegetarian. We didn't, but I've made sure that we have ever since. It just so happened a couple of days before the next festival, my good friend Jens called and asked if I could use some zucchini. I said "Bring it on" and here is the result.

(serves 8-12)

- 2 tbl. olive oil
- 8 oz. fresh button mushrooms, sliced
- 2 stalks celery, chopped
- 1 green pepper, chopped
- 1 large onion, chopped
- 10 garlic cloves, minced
- 2 jalapeno peppers, stemmed, seeded and diced
- 1 tbl. Creole seasoning
- 3-14 1/2 oz. cans Mexican stewed tomatoes
- 1-28 oz can diced tomatoes
- 8-10 10" zucchini, sliced lengthwise in half
- Creole seasoning
- 3 cups rice, cooked according to package directions

Preheat BBQ grille. Heat oil in a large heavy bottomed pot on medium heat. Add mushrooms, celery, onion, garlic, and jalepenos. Stir fry for about 5 minutes or until the mushrooms begin to lose their water. Add 1 tbl. Creole seasoning and mix thoroughly. Add crushed and stewed tomatoes including juice. Simmer 15 minutes stirring occasionally. Meanwhile, sprinkle zucchini with Creole seasoning. Grill on both sides until slightly charred. Slice into bite sized pieces. Add to pot. Bring to a simmer. Serve over cooked rice.

Gerda's Potato Salad

Everybody loves their mom's potato salad and I'm no exception. Mom made hers with fresh items from her garden and it was always great. When Brenda and I got married, we whipped up a batch for our guests. I've tinkered a little bit with it over the years (sorry mom) but basically it's still mom's. (Now you'll be lovin' my mom's potato salad.)

(serves 12-16)

- 5 lbs. Russet or Idaho potatoes
- 1 dozen large eggs
- 1 small red onion, diced fine
- 4 large stalks celery, diced fine
- 2-3 large dill pickles, diced fine
- 6 radishes, sliced thin 4 garlic cloves, minced
- 1 1/2 cups mayonnaise
- 1/3-1/2 cup yellow or Dijon mustard
- Salt and fresh ground black pepper

Peel potatoes and dice into 3/4 inch pieces. Boil until just tender. Drain and cool completely. Boil eggs until hard boiled and allow to cool. Separate yolks from whites and place yolks in a medium size bowl. Mash yolks into small pieces and stir in garlic, mayonnaise and mustard. Chop whites into small even pieces and add to a large mixing bowl. Stir in potatoes, onion, celery and pickles. Gently stir in mayonnaise mixture until well combined. Season with salt and pepper to taste. Refrigerate for 3-4 hours. Potato salad like this tastes best when served very cold. Thanks Mom!!!

Fresh Green Beans with Red Onions and Bacon

We catered a wedding not long ago for a wonderful couple, Robert and Marilyn. Robert asked me to make Kansas City style ribs and we decided to serve garlic smashed potatoes and these green beans as an accompaniment. Brenda was in charge of serving the beans. I think we made a hundred or so servings. I wasn't watching, so after we had served up 50 or so, we were out of the beans. Well, at least the wedding party ate first.

(serves 4-6)

2 lbs. fresh green beans
6 strips of bacon, fried, drained, and diced

1/2 red onion, diced
4 tbl. butter

Either steam or boil beans until just tender, 15-20 minutes and drain. In a large bowl, add beans, bacon, onion, and toss with butter until butter is melted. Serve immediately while beans are still hot. If you like a little spice add some red pepper flakes at the end.

New Potatoes and Creamed Peas

Boy, I love this dish. Growing up, Dad would plant potatoes religiously on Good Friday (although, he really wasn't that religious). As soon as the sweet peas were ready to pick, he would be out digging up fresh new potatoes. Usually most would still be small and very tender. MMMM! Talk about eating good!

(serves 4-6)

2 lbs. fresh small potatoes
2 cups fresh or frozen peas
8 green onions, white and bottom green parts only, sliced fine

2 tbl. butter
2 tbl. flour
2 cups whole milk
Salt and fresh ground black pepper

Wash and scrub potatoes. If some potatoes are large, just cut them in two. Boil potatoes for 10 minutes and add peas. Cook until potatoes are just tender, about 6-8 minutes longer. Drain. While potatoes are cooking, saute onions in butter until softened and tender over medium heat. Add flour and stir for 2 minutes. Add milk. Stir until sauce thickens. When it becomes bubbly, add salt and pepper to taste. Stir for one or two more minutes. Add to potatoes and peas. Heat the mixture thoroughly and serve immediately.

Brenda's Fresh Dressed Cucumbers and Onions

When cucumbers are in season there is always a bowl of Brenda's famous cukes at our house. A very simple and easy to make dish, but just delicious. Personally, I like to add some fresh minced garlic.

4 large cucumbers
1 small white onion
White vinegar
Water

Salt and fresh ground black pepper
Garlic powder or fresh minced garlic (1-2 cloves, if desired)

Wash and peel cucumbers. Slice into 1/8 inch slices. Peel onion and slice in half from top to bottom. Put flat side of onion down on cutting board and slice thin. In a medium sized bowl, add cucumbers and onion. Add white vinegar to cover. Top off with about 1/2 cup cold water. Add salt, pepper, and garlic to taste. Place in refrigerator to chill for an hour or so. Great just out of the bowl or as a sandwich topping.

Big Daddy Lives in Our Hearts Forever

I think love of great barbeque and generosity to your fellow mankind are two wonderful attributes to have in life. And nobody epitomized it more than "Ike" Issac Seymour, better known as "Big Daddy." His barbeque and homemade sauces are still legendary in the state of Iowa.

But his generosity is what always made him my hero. He donated thousands of dollars to the Iowa Food Bank, helped needy elementary school children with clothes and meals, had Thanksgiving turkeys on the tables of the less fortunate, and the list goes on and on. He would raise money for the food bank by challenging people to eat a sandwich with his special sauce in 10 minutes. If a person could eat the entire fiery sandwich Big Daddy would fix a meal for the dollar amount they bet. If not, their money would go to his favorite charity. Only two people, as far as I know, ever finished the sandwich.

I only met Big Daddy a few times when my buddy, Bruce, would take me to Big Daddy's restaurant in Des Moines for some BBQ. One day Ike came up to me with a twinkle in his eye and said "Try this!" On the tip of a plastic knife, he had a little of his latest concoction. I tasted it and said "Well, that's not extremely hot." In a matter of a minute or so, tears were rolling down my cheeks and I literally could not speak. Ike was rolling in laughter. But soon he had a big piece of blueberry cobbler in front of me to cool the heat. What a prankster! And what a wonderful human being. Big Daddy has since passed on, but-thank you, Big Daddy, from all of us whom you touched.

Jim's BBQ Chicken Wings

I usually to make most foods from scratch. However, due to my tight schedules, I don't always have time. So we're going to cheat just a little, but you'll love the results. I use commercially made barbeque sauce and salsa for this dish. But it draws raves and "how did you make this" all of the time. My choices are Open Pit BBQ sauce and Pace medium picante sauce. However, I wouldn't be afraid to go with your favorites. Check it out!

3 lbs. chicken drummettes
Mrs. Dash
3 cloves garlic, minced

6 oz. your favorite BBQ sauce
6 oz. medium picante sauce
Juice of 1/2 large lemon

Preheat oven to 325 degrees. Place drummettes in single layers in a baking dish or two. Sprinkle with Mrs. Dash. Bake 20 minutes. Turn drummettes over, sprinkle with Mrs. Dash, and bake another 20-30 minutes until chicken starts to brown and is cooked through. Mix garlic, BBQ sauce, picante sauce, and lemon juice. Place drummettes on a preheated grill and brown one side. Flip over and brush browned side with sauce. When second side is browned, turn once more, and brush on sauce. Take off grill when pieces are done. Place large bowl or crock-pot. Cover with remaining sauce.

Chef's note: Drummettes are the large part of the three sections of wing and looks like a chicken drumstick.

Kansas City Style Back Baby Ribs

Ribs really need to be cooked a long time to make them nice and tender. In Kansas City, they are slow cooked for up to 10 hours in never more than 225 degree heat. I know of restaurants and people at home who boil their ribs to tenderize them. I, however, like to bake my ribs. I prefer this to boiled ribs. Get ready for some lip smackin' goodies.

(serves 4)

4-5 lbs. baby back pork ribs with silver skin removed

Dry Rub Ingredients

- 1/4 cup light brown sugar packed
- 3 tbl. paprika
- 1 tbl. chili powder
- 1 tbl. kosher salt
- 3 tsp. garlic powder
- 2 tsp. onion powder
- 2 tsp. dry mustard powder
- 2 tsp. fresh ground black pepper

Wet Sauce Ingredients

- 2 cups ketchup
- 1/4 cup apple cider vinegar
- 3 tbl. light molasses

Preheat oven to 275 degrees. Combine dry rub ingredients. Save 1/4 cup. Rub ribs with remainder and bake covered for about 2 hours or until tender. Preheat grill to med/low heat. In a small sauce pan, stir wet sauce ingredients and remaining rub over med/low heat. Simmer about 10 minutes. Place ribs on grill and brush with wet sauce. Grill and turn about every 10 minutes and repeat with brushing with sauce (2 complete turns). Serve immediately.

Teriyaki Lime Wings

I was at one of the local grocery stores not too long ago, and Dave, one of the butchers, asked me if I could use 40 pounds of chicken wings which they got in by mistake. I said "Sure, why not, I'm always up for cooking large." We cooked them at Tom and Theresa's bar and gave them away. 20 pounds were Jim's BBQ wings and for the other 20 pounds I made up following recipe. The Norwegians thanked me.

1 10 oz. bottle teriyaki sauce
5 oz. honey
1/2 tsp. toasted sesame oil
1 tsp fresh ginger, diced fine
1 lime
4 lbs. chicken wings
red pepper flakes

In a food processor or blender, combine teriyaki sauce, honey, sesame seed oil, ginger and garlic. Add the juice of one lime. Process until smooth. Separate chicken into a drumstick and a wingette (cut through the joint at the big section). Add chicken to a large bowl, pour marinade over, and mix thoroughly. Refrigerate 4-8 hours or overnight. Place chicken in a shallow roasting pan. Preheat oven to 325 degrees. Bake chicken 50-60 minutes until wings are cooked through. (Clear liquid will run out when you pierce the larger pieces with a knife). You can serve these now or throw them on your barbeque for nice finish.

Prosciutto Wrapped Shrimp (Devils on Horseback)

A lot of restaurants serve these using bacon as the wrap. I prefer prosciutto, which is an Italian type ham that is sliced thin and has an exquisite flavor. Make sure to stay on top of these once they are on the grill. Keep turning the shrimp, they cook quickly and if you overcook them, they will turn tough.

(Appetizers for 8)

24 large shrimp (20-30 count)
6-8 oz. thin sliced prosciutto
1 cup mayonnaise
1/4 cup chili sauce

2 tbl. finely diced dill pickles
2 tbl. finely diced onion
1 tbl. coarse ground dark mustard
Salt and freshly ground black pepper

Portion prosciutto into sizes to wrap around shrimp, cutting where necessary. Wrap each shrimp with prosciutto and pin with a toothpick. Next, mix remaining ingredients and chill. Light up the barbeque grill. Make sure the cooking surface is very clean so shrimp do not stick. Grill shrimp over medium to medium high heat, turning often for 2-3 minutes until shrimp turns pink. Serve immediately with chilled sauce. You can make individual plates or just let everyone have at it.

Bruce's Grilled Oysters in the Shell

I stood up for Bruce and Lynn's wedding in 1978. They gave me a bottle of Crown Royal as a wedding party gift. I told them I'd save it for their 25th anniversary. And believe it or not, I did. They were living in Post Falls, Idaho, at the time of their 25th anniversary. Brenda and I and the Crown Royal safely secured, arrived to help cook for the festivities. Bruce shared his knowledge of grilling oysters and we all shared the Crown Royal. It was wonderful. Here is my version.

(serves 4-6)

1/4 lb. butter
1 clove garlic minced
Fresh ground black pepper

Fresh squeezed lemon (optional)
24 fresh oysters in the shell

Fire up your grill (gas or charcoal) to medium to medium high heat. In a small sauce pan, melt butter and mix garlic and black pepper to taste. Scrub oyster shells to get rid of grit. Place on preheated grille and cook until oysters open. This could take from 2-10 minutes depending on the oyster. When oysters open, use oven mitts to remove from grille. Use a small paring knife to detach oyster from shell. Try to save as much juice as possible. Add a little butter mixture and lemon juice if desired. Down the hatch, mateys!!! Delicious!

Chef's note: Just take a cooled shell and let oyster slide into one's mouth and swallow.

Mac's Country Style Ribs

Talk about melt in your mouth. I have been making these for at least twenty five years. Always the same, always just delectable. This is a meaty rib dish, which sometimes can have a lot of fat on from the butcher. Feel free to trim the fat. Baking will also take care of a lot of the remaining fat. I cheat a little on this recipe and use a couple commercially made products for the sauce as I do on the chicken wings but they are indeed scrumptious.

(serves 6)

4 lbs. bone on country style pork ribs
Mrs. Dash Original Seasoning
4 cloves garlic, minced

8 oz. your favorite BBQ sauce
8 oz. medium picante sauce
Juice of 1 medium lemon

Preheat oven to 325 degrees. Lightly grease a large baking dish. Place ribs in a single layer in a baking dish. Sprinkle with Mrs. Dash. Bake for one hour. Turn ribs over and sprinkle with Mrs. Dash. Bake for another hour or until meat is very tender. Get the BBQ grille ready to go while ribs are baking. Mix garlic, BBQ sauce, picante sauce, and lemon juice. Grill ribs on one side until nicely browned, about 3-4 minutes. Turn over and brush with sauce. Grill an additional 3-4 minutes and turn again and brush on some more sauce. Grill 4 more minutes and serve.

Erik's Smoked Chicken\
Erik's Blackened Salmon

My good friend Erik lived with Brenda and I on weekends while he worked on the road for three years. We both had sons in high school that were great friends. On weekends we'd get cooking for these boys and their friends. I'd be working on something new to cook during the week and Erik would be working on something to smoke. So "Mad Mac" and "Smoking Ole" (Erik's nickname) would just hunker down and feed a great bunch of boys. What a lot of fun. Here are two of my favorite "Smoking Ole" recipes courtesy of Erik in his own words.

Smoked Chicken

- 1 Brinkman type smoker
- Lots of sugar maple (wood should be green)
- 6 cluckers (chickens)
- Lots of Old Bay seasoning
- Lots of Kikkoman Teriyak1 (the heavy glazing)

Put three cluckers on the bottom smoker tray. Cover the heavy or thickened teriyaki. Shake Old Bay heavy over the whole clucker. Repeat with the top tray. Smoke heavy for 1 1/2 hours. It will be perfect. Stuff the bird if you like with onions or apples.

Blackened Salmon

Did this just this weekend. GET FRESH FISH!!! 3/4 inch steaks or fillets. Big cast iron skillet. Big gas burner. (the outside type like you deep fry a turkey on). Put skillet on burner. No oil in skillet. When skillet gets white hot (10 minutes), take salmon steaks and dredge them in melted butter. Shake Chef Prudhommes blackened red fish seasoning on both sides of fillet. Toss in skillet and watch everyone's mouth drop. The smoke is unbelievable. (Jim's note: only do this outside). 2 1/2 minutes a side- no less. I repeat: don't take the fillet off before 2 1/2 minutes per side. You're going to, but you'll learn. Cook only 2 pieces of fish at a time. The skillet needs to reheat each time you reload it.

Erik's note: "We not only fed these great young men food for their bodies, but we also set great examples- exemplary examples of what type of men we hoped they would grow up to be. We found fun and joy in all we did. Cooking, kids; Jim, it was a wonderful time for all of us.

Alias "Smoking Ole"

Grilled Garlic Lime Chicken with Aluminum Foil Fresh Potatoes

And now for something completely different!! Well Monty Python I'm not, but I'm sure the cast would have enjoyed this. Use some waxy potatoes, like Yukon Golds, which work very well here. The mushrooms just add a great dimension of flavor.

(serves 8)

- 8 chicken breasts, skinned/ boned
- 1 cup soy sauce
- 1/2 cup fresh lime juice
- 2 tbl. Worcestershire sauce
- 1/2 red onion, sliced thin
- 3 garlic cloves, minced
- 1 tsp mustard powder
- Fresh ground black pepper

- 3 lbs. Yukon Gold potatoes
- 1 med. red onion, diced
- 12 oz. fresh button mushrooms, sliced
- 2 green peppers, diced
- 4 garlic cloves, minced
- 1/4 lb. stick butter
- Salt fresh ground black pepper

Combine soy sauce, lime, Worcestershire, onion, garlic, and mustard for a marinade. Place chicken in a shallow baking dish and add marinade. Cover and refrigerate for 1 hour minimum, turning once. Meanwhile, parboil potatoes until barely tender 15-20 minutes. Drain and let cool. Preheat grill to medium. Dice potatoes into 3/8 inch cubes. Mix with remaining vegetables. Place a wide sheet of heavy duty aluminum foil on counter about 24 inches long. Spread potato mixture in center leaving a 1 1/2 inch edge all around. Thin slice butter over top of potato mixture. Cover with same size aluminum foil and crimp edges together well. Place on cookie sheet and then on grill. Roast 20 minutes. Using oven mitts place another cookie sheet on top and turn. Place chicken on grill and cook until done, about 6 minutes a side. Serve it up!!

Marinated Ribeyes with Fresh Grilled Sweet Corn and Chile Butter

Where's the beef? Well it's right here. It's always a little tricky to cook steaks on the grill and get everyone's preferred doneness cooked at the same time. It's a bit of a trial and error thing depending on how hot your grill is. Rule of thumb for a 1 inch thick steak, 4 minutes a side on medium high heat for medium rare. Steaks will keep cooking once off the grill so try to time all at once and put the most well done steaks on first.

(serves 4)

4 8-10 oz. ribeye steaks
6 oz. teriyaki sauce
2 garlic cloves, minced
8 ears fresh sweet corn, husked

1/4 lb. butter
1 1/2 tbl. fresh squeezed lime juice
1/4 tsp. ground red cayenne pepper

Marinate steaks for 1-4 hours with teriyaki and garlic in the refrigerator. When ready to cook, preheat grille to medium high. In the meantime, melt butter and add lime juice and red cayenne pepper. Place steaks on grille in order of doneness preferred (see above). Sweet corn will take about 8 minutes to grill. When ready, place corn ears on grill and turn frequently. Sweet corn is ready when it is dark brown on all sides. You'll get some charring, but try to keep it to a minimum. Plate up steaks and corn. Pass the butter for the corn. Oh man, talk about out of sight!!

My Favorite Irish Joke

A young Irishman sat at a pub in the New World drinking beer and conversin' with the barkeep. Another comes in and sits besides him. He says how you do and hears the lilt and says you be Irish? Yes I am.

The first man yells barkeep give us another round and one for my friend here he's from the mother country as well.

The second man asks-so where in the old country ye from. Dublin responds the first. Dublin you say - so am I and the second man hollers barkeep bring us another round and a shot of your best Irish Whiskey for me and my friend here.

Afterwards the first man asks from where in Dublin and the second man responds with the street and the first man says well I'll be - so am I and yells barkeep another pair of beers and Irish Whiskey for the pair of us.

The phone behind the bar rings and the barkeep answers it. The owner of the pub asks - how is business. The barkeep responds - not too bad - The McCaffery twins are here getting drunk again.

Little Italy

When the moon hits your eye like a big pizza pie that's amore. And it's been an amore affair with Italian cuisine in the Midwest for over a half of a century. Actually, Italians started immigrating to the United States in the late 1890s. But, when the G.I.s returned en masse after World War II, the pepperoni began to fly, the sauces started succulently simmering, and the pastas proudly presented pleasure to the palates of the people.

The macaroni revolution made a marathon plunge into the midlands and forever changed the culinary landscape. The Italians had it down. They had taken what was thought to be an evil and poisonous fruit and transformed it into sauces that begged for infamy. The tomato, which originally came from the Americas, returned in full glory accompanied by garlic and fresh herbs like basil and oregano. So what happened when this wonderful cuisine embraced by thousands of America's finest returning from the Italian front infused into the heartland's abundant harvest of grains, meats, and produce? The breadbasket of America opened it's horn and poured out pestos, pizzas, and pastas that rivaled the old country. Now, that's amore!!!

Basic Red Sauce

What a wonderful combination of just a few ingredients. Fresh tomatoes are the best of course, but canned always work too. If you get in a pinch, you can always use canned sauce. There are some very good tomato sauces on the market, so if time is a constraint, just use your favorite and add the rest of the ingredients.

10 lbs. really ripe tomatoes
2 large white onions, chopped
4 garlic cloves, minced
1 large carrot, peeled and diced
3 tbl. olive oil

12 fresh basil leaves, shredded
Salt and fresh ground black pepper to taste

Wash and core tomatoes. Submerge in boiling water for 30 seconds. Run cold water over and remove skins. Quarter and place in large pot along with onions, garlic, carrot, and olive oil. Simmer for 1 1/2 hours. Puree in a food processor or blender and return to pot. Add basil, salt and pepper and cook down to desired thickness on simmer. Let cool. Place in freezer bags with your usual serving size. Put in freezer and enjoy all year.

Easy Lasagna/Easy Garlic Bread

Okay, Brenda orders lasagna every time we go to an Italian restaurant. Well, maybe not every time, but she really enjoys it. At the Cafe' Deluxe, we never had the same lunch special in a 60 day period. But whenever we served lasagna, we would double the amount of normal servings, just to satisfy the demand. Add a little Ceaser salad and easy garlic bread, It definitely has Brenda's seal of approval.

(serves 10-12)

- 9 lasagna noodles (cooked according to package directions)
- 1 lb. cooked and drained ground beef or Italian sausage
- 1 red onion, diced
- 2 cloves garlic, diced
- 32 oz. tomato sauce
- 2 oz. fresh basil, shredded
- Salt and fresh ground black pepper to taste
- 16 oz. ricotta cheese
- 16 oz. mozzarella cheese, shredded
- 2 oz. grated parmesan cheese
- 1 loaf rustic french bread
- 1/2 cup extra virgin olive oil
- 2 garlic cloves, minced

Preheat oven to 350. Combine meat, onion, garlic, tomato sauce, basil, salt, and black pepper. Spread a little sauce on the bottom of a 15 x 9 greased baking pan. Cover with 3 noodles. Spread 1/3 of sauce over. Spread 1/3 of ricotta cheese over. Spread 1/3 of mozzarella over. Repeat twice and top with parmesan cheese. Bake for one hour. Let stand for 15 minutes. Slice bread in half the long way. Heat olive oil and garlic in small pot. Spread over bread and bake the last 10-15 minutes of lasagna cooking time until golden brown. Slice and serve.

Pizza Time

We always have a crowd at our house on Sundays. If pizza is on the menu, somehow the word gets out and people come out of the woodwork. It's great. There is nothing to be intimidated about here. It is really simple to make. Your whole clan can make it a family thing. It's so much fun when everybody gets involved. Your family may never order pizza again.

Makes 2-12" round pizzas

2 cups basic red sauce (page 102)
2 oz. sliced pepperoni
1 lb. fresh bulk Italian sausage, mild or hot
12 oz. fresh grated mozzarella cheese
1/2 medium red onion, sliced thin
8 oz. mushrooms, sliced thin
Extra virgin olive oil
Salt
Fresh ground black pepper
Fresh grated Parmesan cheese

Dough

1 1/4 oz. package dry yeast
1 1/3 cups 85 degree water
4 cups sifted white all purpose flour
4 tbl. olive oil
1 tsp. salt

Make dough: Dissolve yeast in water until bubbly. Add rest of ingredients. Mix and then knead on floured counter for 10 minutes, adding a little flour if dough is sticky. Place large oiled bowl and cover tightly with plastic wrap. Let rise until double, 1 1/2-2 hours. Punch down and let rise again. Meanwhile, saute mushrooms in 1 tbl. olive oil until they start to brown. Drain and set aside. Brown Italian sausage until cooked thoroughly, drain and set aside. Refrigerate sausage and mushrooms if made ahead of time. Preheat oven to 475 degrees. Divide dough in half. Flour counter and roll dough into a 12" circle. Place on 12" oiled or cornmeal sprinkled round pizza pan. Add 1/2 sauce and spread evenly over dough. Repeat with 1/2 of remaining ingredients. Repeat with 2nd pizza. Bake until crust and cheese is golden brown, 15-20 minutes.

Shrimp Pizza

There is a wonderful restaurant/bar on Highway 35, just 2 miles North of De Soto, Wisconsin. A nice homey outdoorish establishment called, "The Great River Roadhouse." They serve up lots of good stuff, but my favorite is their shrimp pizza. MMM-MMM. This pizza doesn't use a red sauce. It certainly can stand on it's own. Here is my version. MMM-MMM.

(serves 2-3)

4 tbl. olive oil
4 cloves garlic, minced
8 oz. sliced provolone or mozzarella cheese
2 Roma tomatoes, diced
1/2 red onion, sliced into thin rings

1/2 lb. count shrimp, peeled and deveined
8 fresh basil leaves, chopped
Fresh grated Parmesan cheese
1 prebaked 12" pizza crust, homemade or store bought

Preheat oven to 450 degrees. Combine olive oil and garlic. Spread over pre-baked crust with a pastry brush. Cover crust with cheese. Spread shrimp, chopped tomatoes, onion rings, and basil over the top of the cheese. Bake for about 10 minutes. Shrimp should be pink. Try not to overcook or shrimp will get tough.

Chef's note: Recipe for pizza dough is on the previous page. If using homemade dough, you will need to pre-bake it because the shrimp cooks quickly. Roll out dough and place on an oiled pizza pan. Use a fork to pin prick the dough. Bake 5 minutes and flip over. Bake another 5 minutes. Make sure to wear oven mitts so you do not burn yourself.

Seafood Manicotti

You know, there are just some days that you want to do something special for your significant other, or maybe not. Well, if you're in the mood, here's a wonderful little recipe to put him or her in the mood. A little candlelight, background music, and perhaps some white wine.

(serves 8-10)

Manicotti

- 24 manicotti noodles
- 1 lb. cooked shrimp, diced
- 1 lb. lumpcrab meat (make sure to check for shell pieces)
- 2 lbs. cream cheese
- 4 oz. Parmesan cheese
- 6 oz. mozzarella cheese
- 16 oz. ricotta cheese
- Juice of 1 lemon
- 1/2 small red onion, minced
- 3 cloves garlic, minced
- 2 oz. fresh basil, shredded

Cheese Sauce

- 1/4 cup butter
- 3 tbl. flour
- 3 cups milk
- 1/2 tsp. salt
- White pepper to taste
- 1/2 cup parmesan cheese
- 1 bunch green onions

Manicotti

Cook noodles according to package directions. Drain and cool off with cold water. Preheat oven to 350 degrees. Combine remaining manicotti ingredients in a mixer if you have one. If not, do it by hand, but make sure to mix thoroughly. Stuff noodles with mixture. Put a little cheese sauce in the bottom of 2 15 x 9 baking dishes. Divide stuffed noodles between baking dishes and cover with remaining sauce. Bake for 15 minutes or until sauce is bubbly. Serve immediately.

Cheese Sauce

Melt butter in a 2 quart pot. Over medium heat, add flour and stir until it starts to bubble. Slowly add milk and keep stirring until it starts to thicken. Remove from heat and add salt, pepper and parmesan cheese. Dice the bottom green part of the onions and add to sauce.

Chicken Cacciatori

I really like how the different flavors in this dish come together. Known as Hunter's Stew in Italy, I hardly ever see it made with game. The simmering chicken just fills the house with a wonderful aroma. Use regular size spaghetti noodles. It's bold and hearty, and the bigger noodles serve it well.

(serves 8-10)

- 1 cup unbleached white flour
- 2 tsp. salt
- 1/2 tsp. fresh ground pepper
- 2-2/3-4 lb. cut up chickens
- Olive oil
- 1-28 oz. can whole tomatoes
- 1 can 15 oz. tomato sauce
- 8 oz. fresh button mushrooms, sliced thin
- 1 can (6 oz. when drained) pitted black olives, drained
- 2 red onions, diced
- 4-6 cloves garlic, minced
- 2 tsp. salt
- 2 tsp. dried oregano
- Fresh ground black to taste
- 1 lb. spaghetti noodles, cooked according to package directions, drained, and tossed with olive oil

Mix flour, salt, and pepper. Dredge chicken in flour and brown in batches in olive oil in a large skillet. Place in large pot. Mix remaining ingredients in large bowl, breaking up tomatoes. Pour over chicken and bring to a simmer. Cover and cook until thickest pieces of chicken are cooked through, about 25-30 minutes. Immediately serve over noodles with some good garlic bread.

American-Italian Spaghetti

Talk about fusion cooking. This is straight out of 1950's Americana. My mom was a war bride from Germany. She and my dad settled in Cedar Rapids, Iowa. Someone gave them a copy of either *Better Homes and Gardens or The Betty Crocker Cookbook* (I'm not sure, we can't find the cookbook anymore). This is a version of the recipe in it. I grew up on this stuff thinking it was what real spaghetti was. I loved it. It's funky, but your kids will love it and it's a snap to make.

(serves 4-6)

- 2 tbl. extra virgin olive oil
- 1 small yellow onion, diced
- 4 oz. fresh button mushrooms, sliced
- 1 garlic clove, minced
- 1 lb. fresh ground beef
- 1-10 oz. can condensed tomato soup
- 1-10 oz. can condensed cream of mushroom soup
- 6-8 drops Tabasco sauce
- 1-8 oz. package spaghetti noodles
- Fresh grated Parmesan cheese

Saute onions, mushrooms, and garlic until mushrooms are start to lose their water (about 3-4 minutes). Drain and set aside. Brown ground beef in large skillet. Drain. Mix sauteed vegetables, ground beef, tomato and mushroom soup and Tabasco sauce. Bring to a simmer. Meanwhile, cook noodles according to package directions and drain. Plate up noodles and spread sauce over. Sprinkle with Parmesan cheese. Enjoy a blast from the past.

Cappellini

So, you just want something light, refreshing, and hardly any time in the kitchen? Look no further. By the time your noodle water is boiling, all of your ingredients can be prepared. It makes my mouth water just thinking about it. The sauce comes together quick, so if you would like to add some shrimp, add it right when you start the sauce. (I sometimes add flaked red pepper just to spice it up.)

(serves 4)

- Extra virgin olive oil
- 4-5 large fresh from the garden tomatoes, diced
- 1/2 medium red onion, diced
- 2 cloves garlic, minced
- 1/4 cup unpacked fresh basil leaves
- Salt
- Fresh ground black pepper
- 1 lb. uncooked 30-40 count shrimp (optional), peeled and deveined
- 6 oz. angel hair pasta

Start pasta water immediately. In a large skillet, saute tomatoes, onions, and garlic 3-4 minutes in 1-2 tbl. olive oil. Add basil and saute 30 seconds more. Salt and pepper to taste. If using shrimp, cappellini sauce is ready when shrimp turns pink. At the same time, cook noodles according to package directions and drain. Serve sauce over top of noodles immediately for best results. This truly is a dish where some good rustic garlic bread is great to mop up any remaining sauce on one's plate.

Italian Gravy

George & Sharon have been great friends of ours for years. George is of Greek descent and Sharon of Norwegian. George asked if I'd help him come up with a couple of dishes to represent both, for a family reunion dinner they were in charge of. We made gyros and Norwegian meatballs.

We also made some new acquaintances. Jerry came over and introduced himself. He is a retired coach from Central Iowa and started regaling me with tales of his mom and grandma making ravioli and drying it all over the house on newspapers, beds, everything. He also told me of this wonderful sauce he and his wife Cheryl make to this day.

Here it is, as described by Cheryl. Thanks Jerry and Cheryl !!!

1/2 cup olive oil (4 oz.)
4 ribs celery, chopped
1 large onion, chopped
Handful dried mushrooms

1 small can tomato paste
5 cans water
Garlic salt to taste
Salt and pepper to taste

Soak mushrooms in warm water. (Cover for a 1/2 hour at least). Heat oil, add celery and onion and cook for awhile. Then drain and cut up mushrooms and add to pan. Cook until celery and onions begin to look transparent. Add tomato paste, water, and spices and simmer for 5 hours. Serve on mostaccioli noodles. I sometimes save some of the mushroom water and add to the sauce. It gives it more of a brown look. Also, when I serve a pork roast, I cut the bone off the roast and put the bone in the gravy for the last hour of simmering.

This recipe will only work or I should say taste right with dried mushrooms. This was served every Sunday in my husband's family when he was growing up. The original recipe was brought from Italy by my husband's great grandmother.

Enjoy! Cheryl L.

Shrimp Fettucine for Esther

It was Conor's friend, Esther's, birthday. She comes from a large family in upstate New York with a very Italian father. So when she asked me to make this dish, I knew I had to put out my best effort. It must have cut the mustard, though, because I think she even had thirds.

1 1/2 cups butter, cut into small chunks
3 cups whipping cream or 1/2 and 1/2
Fresh ground black pepper to taste
6 oz. diced prosciutto
1/2 med. red onion, diced
4-5 cloves garlic, minced
1 bunch fresh flat Italian parsley, destemmed and chopped

2 lbs. 30-40 count uncooked shrimp, peeled and deveined
1 oz. fresh basil, diced fine
3 cups fresh grated Parmesan cheese
24 oz. fettucine noodles, cooked and drained
olive oil

In a medium sauce pan, add butter and cream. Stirring frequently, bring to a simmer for 1-2 minutes until it thickens. Add pepper to taste. Stir in red onion, garlic, prosciutto, and parsley. Take off heat and let rest. Bring 3-4 quarts of water to a boil in a large pot. Add shrimp and cook until just pink. Drain and add to sauce along with fresh basil and Parmesan cheese. Combine with fettucine noodles and serve.

Chef's note: While making sauce and shrimp have water boiling for noodles. Cook according to package directions, drain, and toss with olive oil to prevent sticking.

Grin and Beer It

Beer, it's just not for breakfast anymore. Did you hear the one about the Irishman who walked out of a bar? Hey it could happen!

Beer drinking is a huge tradition in the Midwest. Cooking with beer is a much lesser known tradition. However, cooking with beer is often accompanied by drinking the same libation. Results may vary depending on the amount of brew consumed during the cooking process.

Beer has been around for approximately 10,000 years. It is thought that some water and grain fermented under the right conditions and the rest is history. My question is who was the idiot that took the first drink of this fermenting concoction? One can only imagine the smell and appearance of this swill. We all love that idiot and hats off to him from grateful beer drinkers around the world.

Cooking with beer can and will add new dimensions to most of your favorite foods. However, I don't recommend putting it on your cornflakes. And try to refrain from pilsner beer floats. That is just too much of a good time.

"He was a wise man who invented beer" Plato said. This kind of rebuts my idiot theory, but hey, everybody is entitled to their own opinion.

"Beer is proof God loves us and wants us to be happy." — Benjamin Franklin

Guinness and Lamb Irish Stew

The Irish like their lamb and they also like their Guinness. So it's not surprising that somewhere along the way they got paired up in a stew. And a rather wonderful stew at that. If lamb is too strong for you, substitute beef instead. Great on those wintry days.

(serves 12-16)

4 tbl. corn or peanut oil
3 lbs. lamb shoulder, cut into 1" chunks
5 tbl. flour
1 tsp. salt
1/2 tsp. pepper
1/4 tsp. cayenne pepper
1-14.9 oz. can Guinness Stout
4 lbs. russet potatoes, peeled and diced
1 lb. carrots peeled, and chopped
2 large yellow onions, diced
5 cloves garlic, minced
3 quarts beef broth
1 sprig fresh rosemary
1 sprig fresh thyme
Salt and fresh ground black pepper to taste

In a mixing bowl, coat lamb with 1 tbl. oil. Season flour with salt, pepper, and cayenne pepper. Dredge lamb in seasoned flour. Heat remaining oil in a large heavy bottomed skillet. Brown lamb on all sides. Turn off and remove lamb from skillet. Pour Guinness into skillet and turn heat on high. Once the beer is at a boil, use a spatula to scrape up any renderings on the bottom of the skillet. This is known as deglazing. Remove from heat and pour into a large stockpot. Add the lamb, potatoes, carrots, onions, garlic, and beef broth. Bring stew to a low simmer for 1 1/2 hours. Tie rosemary and thyme together. Place in stew with 15 minutes to go. Remove when stew is ready to serve. Add salt and pepper to taste.

"It's the Wurst"

Thanks to all of the sausage makers past and present who gave us their version of the venerable bratwurst. One of the greatest ways I've had a hand in was "Outback" at Tom & Theresa's bar.

We loaded a ten gallon milk can with 30 pounds of bratwurst, 6 quartered large cabbages, 4 quartered large onions and a couple heads of garlic. We added a twelve pack of beer, Then put the lid on, in which a 1" hole had been drilled. We then placed it on top of an outside burner that is used for deep frying turkeys. When steam started blowing through the escape hole, dinner was served. Just to die for. Here's a recipe for home use.

(serves 8)

16 bratwurst
1 large cabbage, quartered
1 large onion, sliced thin

4 cloves garlic in skins
4-12 oz. bottles lager beer
1 tbl. caraway seed (optional)

In a large pot, combine all ingredients. Bring to a boil and simmer gently for about 30 minutes. Bratwurst needs to be cooked thoroughly and cabbage needs to be limp. Drain and remove garlic. Pile cabbage and onions in the center of a large serving platter. Place bratwurst on the outside. Have a few of your favorite mustards to pass around and some cold refreshments to wash these down with. Let the tailgating begin.

Shanon's Premium Beer-battered Fish

Shanon calls his recipe by the above name because he likes to use Grainbelt Premium Beer for his batter. We've tried it with other beers and have gotten similar results. So if Grainbelt isn't available, just use your favorite. I'm sure you'll agree, it's a premium way to fry fish.

(serves 4)

2 lbs. firm white fish such as cod, fresh or thawed, 1/2 inch thick
1 1/2 cups pancake flour
3/4 cup warm beer
3 eggs, well beaten
2 tsp. Cajun seasoning
1 tsp. salt
1 large lemon, wedged
Peanut or corn oil

Mix flour, beer, eggs, Cajun seasoning, and salt in a medium mixing bowl and let rest in the refrigerator 2-4 hours. Pat dry fish with paper towels. Fill a heavy bottomed skillet with 1-1 1/2 inches of oil. Using a candy thermometer bring oil to 350 degrees. Dip fish in beer batter and fry one piece at a time. You will be able to see when the bottom starts to turn brown and it is time to turn fish. Use a tongs. It should take about 1 1/2-2 minutes a side. Drain on paper towels. Keep warm until all fish is cooked. Serve with lemon wedges.

Garlic Beer Fried Chicken

There is a little Chinese restaurant in the Pike Street Market in Seattle which I love to go to for their garlic chicken wings. They are sooo good. In this recipe the chicken is poached in beer, chilled, and later deep fried. It's a totally different version but I like it just as well.

(Makes appetizers for 8-10)

- 4 lbs. chicken wings, washed and patted dry
- 4-12 oz. beers
- 2 large eggs
- 1/2 cup beer
- 2 tbl. soy sauce
- 3 tbl. garlic salt
- 1/2 cup flour
- 1/2 cup cornstarch
- 1 tsp. baking powder
- 1/2 tsp. fresh ground black pepper
- Peanut or corn oil

Place chicken in large pot. Pour 4 beers over. If necessary, add water so liquid is at least 1 inch above chicken. Par boil until chicken is cooked through. Drain and chill about 2 hours. Stir remaining ingredients until smooth. Add chicken and mix with wooden spoon until well coated. Heat oil to 360-370 degrees in large heavy bottomed skillet. Fry chicken in batches until golden brown Drain on paper towels and serve it up. Oh Yeah.

Beer and Cheese Fondue

Have you heard? Fondue is back, alive and kicking. Try this at your next fondue soiree. With fondue it's always important to have a good quality bread for dipping. I like to go for Artisan baked rustic type breads from good bakeries. You usually can find something even at your local grocery.

- 1-12 oz. warm beer
- 2 garlic cloves, minced
- 1/2 red pepper, diced fine
- 1/2 cup red onion, diced fine
- 3 cups shredded Swiss cheese
- 1 1/2 cups sharp shredded cheddar cheese
- 2 tbl. flour
- 1 tbl. Worchestershire sauce
- 6-8 drops cayenne pepper sauce
- 1 loaf rustic bread, cubed
- Bite sized veggies, like broccoli and cauliflower

It is very important not to let the cheese boil. You want it to melt and thicken only. Bring beer to a simmer over low heat or in a double boiler. Add garlic, red pepper, and onion. Add 1 tbl. flour to each of the cheeses and mix in. In small batches, slowly add cheeses to beer mixture, stirring constantly. Do not let boil or the cheese will separate. Add Worchestershire and cayenne sauces. Transfer to a fondue pot or a crockpot on warm. Pass around the bread and veggies for dipping. Apple slices are a hit with this dish also. Have fun!!!

Grilled Pork Chops and Bavarian Beer Sauce with a Spaetzle Side

Fire up the barbeque. You're going to love these. You can use any type of pork chop you like. Brenda and I tend to go for thin cut chops, but this sauce will enhance whatever you use.

Spaetzle is a type of German dumpling which is very easy to make and becomes a great accompaniment to the sauced pork. Hey, put some of that sauce on the spaetzle too!

(serves 4)

4-12 oz. pork chops, grilled

Bavarian Beer Sauce

1 tbl. butter
1 tbl. flour
1/2 large onion, diced fine
1/2 cup dijon mustard

1/2 cup honey
3 cups wheat beer
2 tbl. red wine vinegar

In a small 8-10 cup pot, melt butter. Add flour and whisk continually for 4-5 minutes over low/medium heat. Be careful not to burn. Turn off heat and add remaining ingredients. Bring to a boil and stir often until thickened.

Spaetzle

2 1/4 cups flour
1 tsp. salt

1 well beaten egg
1/4-3/4 cup water

Combine flour and salt. Blend in egg. Add water slowly until batter thickens but is still smooth. Roll out on a floured surface. Use a knife to make small pieces. Drop a few at a time in boiling salted water for 5-8 minutes until cooked through. Serve with beer sauce or a little melted butter and fresh grated parmesan cheese.

Beer-batter Pancakes

Well, we're not pouring beer over cornflakes this morning. No, we are making pancakes with an attitude. Step up to the challenge. Next time you're making breakfast for your friends or family, try these. If you have real maple syrup, it really goes well on these. A little bacon on the side with some fresh orange juice, and who could want more. Unless, it's seconds, of course.

(serves 6-8)

3 cups flour
3 tsp. baking powder
1 tsp. salt
2 tbl. white sugar

3 large eggs, separated
1 cup beer at room temperature
1 1/2 cups milk
1/3 cup melted butter

In a medium sized bowl, beat egg yolks. Stir in beer, milk, butter, and dry ingredients until smooth. In a another bowl, whisk egg whites until stiff. Fold in batter. On a hot oiled griddle or heavy duty skillet, pour about 1/3 cup to form each pancake. When pancake is full of holes on top flip and cook another 1-2 minutes. Continue until batter is used up. You will probably need to re-oil griddle after each batch. Top with your favorite pancake topping.

Country-style Pork Ribs with Beer Barbeque Sauce

Country style ribs have a lot of meat on the bone. Cooking these ribs with the bone on just enhances the flavor. I never buy boneless country style ribs. I also always prebake my ribs to get them tender before throwing them on the grill. It works great and goes great with the beer BBQ sauce.

(serves 8-10)

5 lbs. country style pork ribs, bone on
Salt and fresh ground black pepper
Cayenne pepper (optional)
1 cup beer
1 cup chili sauce
1/4 cup white wine vinegar

1 medium onion, diced
2 garlic cloves, minced
1/4 cup brown sugar
Juice of 1 lemon
1/8 tsp. cayenne pepper
Salt

Preheat oven to 325 degrees. Salt and pepper ribs on both sides. Bake in oven for about 2 hours until meat is falling off bones. In a large sauce pan, combine beer, chili sauce, and vinegar. Simmer for 5 minutes. Add onions, garlic, sugar, lemon juice, and cayenne. Simmer another 10 minutes. Taste. Add salt if necessary. Transfer cooked ribs to a large platter. On a preheated BBQ grill,e cook ribs over medium heat. Baste with BBQ sauce on one side. Turn in 2-3 minutes and baste the other side. Grill another 2-3 minutes and serve them ribs up!!!

Not Just Your Average Drunken Chicken

Talk about your well sauced chicken. You would be too if you were marinated in beer for two days. I prefer baking my chicken in the oven before putting it on the grill. Precooked like that helps lessen the chances of grease flare-ups and burning the chicken. A nice lively party dish. This goes well with Gerda's Potato Salad (page 84).

(serves 4)

1 fresh chicken, cut in pieces
2- 12 oz. pilsner beers
3 tbl. olive oil
3 tbl. coarse ground brown mustard
1 red onion sliced thin

2 cloves garlic, minced
Cayenne pepper sauce
Salt and fresh ground black pepper

Wash chicken and pat dry. Place in a glass baking dish, 9x13 or larger. Mix beer, oil, and mustard. Pour over chicken. Add onion and garlic and spread around. Add a few drops of cayenne pepper sauce here and there. Add salt and pepper to taste. Cover with plastic wrap and marinate for up to 2 days turning occasionally. Save marinade. Preheat oven to 325 degrees. Bake chicken in marinade for 50-60 minutes or until juices run clear. Finish on the grill, using marinade once on each side.

Marvelous Drunken Beans and Grilled Sausage Delights

Here's a good combo to write home to mom about. If you like beans, these are killer. I recommend you use a good full bodied wheat beer as your base. Get a couple or three pounds each of your favorite sausage and polish kielbasa. And it doesn't hurt to have a beer or two to wash it down with.

(serves 8-10)

- 3 lbs. Polish kielbasa
- 3 lbs. fresh bratwurst
- 3 lbs. hot Italian sausages
- 1 lb. navy or great northern beans, soaked in water overnight
- 2-12 oz. bottles wheat beer
- 2 bay leaves
- 4 cups water
- 3 tbl. olive oil
- 2 red onions, diced
- 3 cloves garlic, minced
- 1 tsp. allspice
- 1 tsp. coriander
- Salt and fresh ground black pepper

Rinse soaked beans. Combine with beer, bay leaves, and water in a large pot. Simmer for 1 1/2 hours until beans are just cooked through. Drain and remove bay leaves. Saute onions and garlic in olive oil and add seasoning. Mix with beans. In the meantime, grill up sausages. Put beans on a large serving platter and arrange sausages over. You can garnish with some fresh parsley if you like.

State Dish of Minnesota

Never let it be said that the good citizens of Minnesota are a few peas short of a full casserole. They just think it adds too much color to the tuna dish. All over Minnesota, at hundreds of church gatherings, potlucks are as entrenched in the tradition and culture as blond hair and Paul Bunyan and "Babe" the Blue Ox. The casserole divas come out in droves to fill up church basements with their favorite concoctions. These are shared and enjoyed communally with other members of their congregations. In Minnesota (actually the only Scandinavian country located within the continental United States) these creations are widely known as "Hot Dish."

And up to a couple years ago, these hotdish happenings were "above the law." It seems that holding these public gatherings with food brought in from non-state inspected kitchens was in violation of food safety ordinances. Mostly, the food police turned a blind eye to these "illegal" activities. However, not always. Al Juhnke, who happened to be a state senator, was turned away at the door of a Democrat/ Farmer/Labor (DFL) gathering and told to take his crockpot back to his car. Annoyed, he got a "Hot Dish" bill passed to exempt organizations potlucks from state food handling regulations. The Sons of Norway rejoiced. No longer were they outlaws in the North Star State.

So have a little fun. Go crazy. Add some green peas to that tuna casserole and maybe even a red pepper or two. You may be the hurrah of the hotdish hullaberoo.

Scalloped Potatoes and Ham

Casseroles are a great way to use up leftovers. Have some Easter ham leftover you want to make an evening family dinner with? This is a very quickly prepared dish that takes about an hour to cook in the oven.

(serves 8-10)

8 med. baking potatoes, sliced thin (about 8 cups)
1 large onion, halved and sliced thin
8 oz. white button mushrooms, sliced thin
3 cups diced ham
Salt

Nutmeg
Fresh ground black pepper
12 oz. shredded Swiss cheese
4 large eggs
3 cups Half and Half

Preheat oven to 350 degrees. Take 1/3 of the potatoes and layer on the bottom of a lightly greased 9 x 15 baking dish. Spread 1/3 of onions, mushrooms and ham over potatoes. Sprinkle with salt, nutmeg and pepper. Cover with 1/3 of the cheese. Repeat twice. Beat eggs in a mixing bowl and stir in 1/2 and 1/2. Pour over potato mixture. Bake 1 to 1 1/2 hours or until cheese and potato mixture is golden brown.

Classic Tuna Casserole with a Little Umph

Every good standing hot dish diva has a few cans of tuna and cream of mushroom soup on hand in their pantry, just in case a quick casserole needs to be thrown together. So let's move beyond adding green peas for color and throw caution to the wind. Let's say "Go have a little fun with tradition."

(serves 10-12)

8 oz. medium egg noodles
2-6 oz. cans tuna in water
1-10 1/2 oz. can condensed cream of mushroom soup
1-10 1/2 oz. can condensed cream of celery soup
1/2 red onion, diced
1/2 red pepper, diced
1 cup fresh or frozen mixed vegetables
2 oz. grated parmesan cheese
12 saltines

Preheat oven to 375 degrees. Boil noodles according to package directions and drain. Place in a large mixing bowl. Drain tuna and add. Add soups, onion, red pepper, and mixed vegetables. Mix well. Pour into a greased 2 quart baking dish. Sprinkle parmesan cheese over. Crush saltines and spread over mixture. Bake uncovered for 30-35 minutes until piping hot.

Here's the Beef with Wild Rice

Yah, you might have had something like this if you come from Northern Minnesota! And if you haven't, check it out.

I always wash my white rice prior to cooking. Put it in a bowl, run cold water over and swirl around with your fingers, drain and repeat 3 or 4 times until water is clear and no longer milky looking. This rinses off the outside starch and keeps the rice from sticking together.

(serves 6-8)

- 2 lbs. round steak, cut into 1 inch pieces
- 2 tbl. corn oil
- 1 red onion, diced
- 3 cloves garlic, minced
- 8 oz. fresh button mushrooms, sliced
- 2 celery stalks, diced
- 3/4 cup white rice
- 3/4 cup wild rice
- 6 oz. fresh or frozen sweet corn kernels
- 2-14 oz. cans beef broth
- 3 tbl. teriyaki sauce

Preheat oven to 350 degrees. Brown steak in oil in a large skillet. Remove from skillet. Add onion, garlic, mushrooms, and celery to skillet and saute 5-6 minutes. Add steak back in along with the rice and corn. Pour in broth and teriyaki sauce and bring to a boil. Grease a 13 x 9 casserole dish and add steak and rice mixture. Bake for 45-50 minutes until is fully cooked. Stir rice with a fork before serving.

Mac's Twisted Greek Lamb Casserole

Traditionally, the dish uses eggplant. However, living in a small town that doesn't necessarily sell enough eggplant to make it profitable to keep them on the shelf year round, forced me to change gears. And change thought patterns.

I substituted squash and zucchini and decided to grill them to bring out their sweetness and here's what we put on the table. Use eggplant if you like, but I'd recommend putting it on the grill. Wow, what flavors!

(serves 10-12)

- 2 tbl. olive oil
- 5-6 cloves garlic, minced
- 1 medium red onion, diced
- 4 5-6" yellow squash
- 4 5-6" zucchini
- 2 lbs. boneless lamb, diced in 3/8" cubes
- 3 tbl. olive oil
- 1 oz. fresh mint
- 1 oz. fresh basil
- 2-3 shoots fresh rosemary
- 2-28 oz. cans crushed tomatoes
- Salt
- Fresh ground black pepper
- 8 oz. farafelle noodles (bowtie)
- 2 cups plain low fat yogurt
- 1/2 cup flour
- 2 large eggs
- 1/2 tsp. salt
- Fresh ground black pepper
- 8 oz. shredded Parmesan cheese

Fire up the grill to high heat or turn on your broiler. Destem squash and zucchini. Slice each lengthways into 4 equal slabs. Throw onto grill and salt and pepper if you like. Grill until slightly charred on both sides. Remove from grill let cool and dice. Set aside. In a Dutch oven, add 2 tbl. olive oil and saute garlic and onion until onion is soft, about 4 minutes. At the same time, saute lamb in 3 tbl. olive oil in a large skillet until browned on all sides. Drain and add lamb and grilled vegetables to garlic and onion mixture in Dutch oven. Chop mint and basil fine. Strip rosemary from shoots. Add herbs to dutch oven. Add crushed tomatoes and simmer 20-30 minutes until lamb is tender. Turn off heat. While sauce is simmering, prepare noodles according to package directions. Drain, add a little olive oil and toss to prevent sticking.

Make the topping. Combine yogurt, flour, eggs, salt and a little fresh ground black pepper. Hand whisk until smooth. Preheat oven to 325 degrees. OK, let's put this together. Make a layer of 1/2 of the noodles on the bottom of a greased 11 X 17 casserole dish. Spread 1/2 of the sauce over noodles. Repeat. Carefully spread topping over, cover with Parmesan cheese and bake until topping is solid and starts to brown. Let set 10 minutes after taking out oven to set up before serving.

Baked Cabbage Rolls with Spicy Tomato Sauce

I just love cabbage rolls, but I probably only get time to make them once or twice a year. Which is too bad, because they are easy, economical and extremely delicious. The spicy tomato sauce just absolutely makes it.

(serves 10-12)

1 lb. ground beef
1 lb. ground pork
Salt and fresh ground black pepper
2/3 cup uncooked rice
1 med. onion, diced
2 cloves garlic, minced
15 oz. can diced tomatoes
15 oz. beef broth (canned or homemade)
1 tsp. dried crushed oregano
2 large heads cored cabbage, outer 2 or 3 leaves removed
28 oz. can tomato sauce
2 cloves garlic, minced
2 tsp. crushed oregano
1 tsp. fresh ground black pepper

Preheat oven to 350 degrees. Brown beef and pork in a large skillet. Salt and pepper to taste. Drain. Put back in skillet and add rice, onion, 2 cloves minced garlic, diced tomatoes, beef broth, and 1 tsp. dried crushed oregano. Bring to boil. Reduce heat and simmer 20 minutes. Take off heat. Boil cabbage heads whole 15 minutes. Remove 12 outer leaves from each head. Put 2 large tbl. meat mixture at stem end of each leaf. Roll up and place in two 9 x 15 baking dishes. Mix tomato sauce, garlic, oregano, and pepper. Pour over cabbage and bake 40 minutes.

Ham & Egg Brunch Casserole

A rather easy and non time consuming way to take care of a crowd over for Sunday morning brunch. Make some toast from some good bread, add some melon and grape salad (page 52), brew some coffee, put out some juice, maybe some mimosas, and you are good to go. This is Fawn's easy breakfast recipe. Thanks Fawn.

(serves 4-6)

- 6 slices whole wheat bread
- 8 oz. cheddar cheese
- 12 large eggs
- 3 tbl. milk
- 4-5 button mushrooms, sliced or diced
- 1/2 red pepper, diced
- 1 small onion, diced
- 6 oz. diced ham

Preheat oven to 375 Degrees. In a 9 x 15 baking dish, cover bottom with bread. Spread 4 oz. of cheddar cheese over bread. In a large bowl, beat eggs and milk. Add mushrooms, red pepper, onion, and ham and mix well. Pour over cheese and bread. Spread remaining cheese over egg mixture. Bake in oven for 35-40 minutes until eggs are cooked and well set.

Potatoes O'Brien Hash Brown Casserole

A little twist on Potatoes O'Brien which are actually diced potatoes with onions and green peppers. I made this for a Mother's Day Brunch. It was just devoured. So simple to make and yet a wonderful dish to grace your table.

(serves 6-8)

- 2 lb. shredded hashbrown potatoes (fresh, or frozen and thawed, and patted dry with paper towels
- 1/2 cup butter, melted
- 1 onion, diced
- 1 green pepper, diced
- 3 garlic cloves, minced
- 16 oz. sour cream
- 1-10 oz. can cream chicken soup
- 8 oz. shredded cheddar cheese
- Salt and fresh ground black pepper to taste

Preheat oven to 350 degrees. Mix all ingredients in a 11' x 17" casserole dish. Bake uncovered 1 to 1 1/2 hours. Pull out of oven and let stand 5-7 minutes. Serve it with the rest of your brunch or just by itself. Enjoy!!

Baked Spaghetti and Basil Meatballs

As you probably can tell, I use a lot of basil. These meatballs are no exception. I make them using hot Italian sausage, but if you prefer a mild sausage, go for it. Make an extra pan for the freezer for the unexpected crowd.

(serves 8-10)

4 oz. spaghetti noodles, cooked according to package directions

3 lbs. ground hot Italian sausage

8 garlic cloves, minced

4 oz. fresh basil, shredded

2 tbl. corn oil

2-28 oz. cans tomato sauce (or homemade, see page 102)

1 medium red onion, diced

Salt and fresh ground black pepper to taste

4 oz. Parmesan cheese

Preheat oven to 350 degrees. Drain spaghetti noodles. Add 1/2 of the garlic and basil to Italian sausage and mix well. Form sausage into golf ball sized balls. Brown in oil in large skillet. Set aside. Add remaining garlic, basil, and the onion to the tomato in a mixing bowl. Stir thoroughly. Salt pepper to taste.

In a 15 x 9 baking dish mix noodles, meatballs, and sauce. Spread cheese over. Bake 30-40 minutes until bubbly and meatballs are cooked through.

Green Salsa, Tortilla and Black Bean Casserole

A little veggie fun south of the border. You could add some cooked ground beef or shredded chicken if you like, but I don't think it's necessary. Great for a main dish or enough for 10-12 side dishes.

- 2 large onions, chopped
- 2 large green peppers, chopped
- 4 cloves garlic, minced
- 1-14 oz. can diced tomatoes
- 1 cup salsa verde (see page 24) or store bought
- 2-3 tsp. cumin

- 3 tbl. olive oil
- 2-15 o.z cans black beans drained (rinse for less sodium)
- 12 oz. shredded Monterey jack cheese
- 6 oz. shredded Parmesan cheese
- 12-6 inch corn tortillas

Optional Toppings

- 2 medium ripe tomatoes, diced
- 2 sliced fresh avocados
- Sliced black or green olives

- Chopped red onion
- 1 cup sour cream or creme freche

Preheat oven to 350 degrees. In large skillet heat olive oil over medium heat. Stir fry onions, green peppers, garlic, tomatoes, salsa, and cumin for 3 minutes. Turn off heat and stir in beans. In a 11" x 17" casserole dish spread 1/3 of bean mixture evenly across bottom. Cover with 1/3 of Monterey jack and Parmesan cheese. Top with 6 tortillas. You will overlap. Repeat for second layer. For the third layer use the remaining bean mixture and cover with remaining cheese. Cover with aluminum foil and bake 30 minutes. Uncover and bake an additional 15 minutes until top cheese is thoroughly melted. Take out of oven and let cool 8-10 minutes. Cut and serve. Pass around optional toppings.

Bowtie Delight

A lot of times the simplest things can create a new favorite. I had some leftover marinated steak and decided to make do with what I had in the pantry and refrigerator. We took it up to Shanon and Morgan's for a little family BBQ. It was devoured in 10 minutes. You can use any steak. Leftovers are great for this. If you want start from scratch, round steak is probably the most economical.

(serves 8-10)

- 1 lb. round steak, cubed into 1/4" x 1/4" pieces
- 3 tbl. teriyaki sauce
- 4 cloves garlic, minced
- 8 oz. farafelle (bowtie) pasta
- 3 bunches green onions, chopped (white and light green parts only)
- 1/3 red onion, diced
- 1/2 large red pepper, diced
- 3-10 oz. cans condensed cream of mushroom soup
- 6 oz. grated sharp cheddar cheese

Marinate steak in teriyaki sauce and 1 clove minced garlic for at least 1 hour or overnight. Saute steak until browned on all sides. Preheat oven to 325 degrees. Make pasta according to package directions. Drain and toss with a little olive oil to prevent sticking. Grease a 9" X 15" casserole dish. Add all remaining ingredients to casserole dish and mix well. Cover with aluminum foil and bake 20-30 minutes until nice and hot. Serve immediately.

Waiter, There's a Fly in My Soup

"Ladies and Gentlemen"

It's time for the greatest soup story ever told. A tale of epic proportions that will embrace the annals of human history until the end of time. So pull up a chair, lend an ear, and I'll regale you with a tale that will warm your heart and certainly give you soup for thought.

Once upon a time, in a faraway land, three soldiers trudged down the road weary and hungry on their way home from war. The village was in the throes of famine. The soldiers asked if anyone had a table that they could have a meal at. The villagers refused, stating they needed what little food they had they to feed their children and the sick. What little seed they had, they needed to plant in the spring.

The three soldiers conferred and said "What we need to do is make stone soup. Does anyone have a large iron pot which we can fill with water and wood to heat it?" When the villagers provided their request, one soldier asked for three smooth round stones. These were furnished and he promptly added them to the pot and brought it to a boil. At once, the soldier tasted it and proclaimed that the wonder of stone soup was not that it feeds hungry people but that brings people together. The villagers had gathered around, eyeing each other quizzically. The soldier asked "Would anyone happen to have a couple of carrots? They always add so much flavor to stone soup." An old woman hesitated and then said "I think I have a couple I can spare."

As the second soldier cut up the carrots and put them into the soup, the third soldier tasted and said "You know this is pretty good but if anyone had a little salt beef, it would certainly add some robustness." The town butcher said he could bring some over. When it was added, the first soldier tasted the broth and declared "I'm starting to really like this soup, but I think it really needs some cabbage." A young girl standing by said she knew her mom had a couple at home and went to fetch them. Once added the second soldier tasted and said "I once made stone for a rich man who had potatoes and a bit of ham." The villagers talked amongst themselves and said if they brought some potatoes and ham, maybe some milk and barley, they could eat like rich people and they did. The men brought in large tables and somehow bread and cider appeared and everyone feasted into the night.

In the morning, the villagers found the soldiers had departed. A young girl stated "Look, the stones are still in the pot and since we know how to make stone soup, we never have to be hungry again." Her grandfather replied "That's true, but remember like the soldier said, it brought us all together." Remember this the next time you make soup. Sometimes the simplest things can bring people together.

*This fable has been told numerous ways for years. This is just a version I put together.

Tortilla Soup

Okay, I know Mazatlan isn't anywhere near the Midwest, but the best tortilla soup I've ever come across is there at the Ancla restaurant located in the Riveria on the Beach Hotel. I'm sitting in the bar writing this, It's the end of February, and the entire state of Minnesota has arrived here.

Ignacio, who used to be the head chef, has since moved on, took the time to write out his recipe for me about four years ago. Of course, it was written in Spanish, so I couldn't read it. I have since had it translated and here is our closest version. Thanks, Meme, for the translation.

- 1/4 cup corn oil
- 2 garlic cloves, minced
- 1 medium onion, diced fine
- 1 teaspoon Mexican oregano
- 1 oz. fresh basil, shredded small
- 1-28 oz. can tomato sauce
- 32 oz. chicken broth
- White pepper to taste
- 24 tortilla chips
- 1 can evaporated milk
- 1 lb. chihuahua cheese, shredded
- 1 chicken seasoning cube (optional)
- 2 avocados peeled and sliced

Saute garlic and onion in oil. Add tomato sauce and chicken broth along with oregano and basil. I don't use the chicken seasoning cube but feel free to if desired. Simmer for twenty minutes. Place three tortilla chips in the bottom of a soup bowl. Add some milk and cheese. Pour soup over the top. Garnish with avocado.

Basic Chili

I made up this recipe for the Cafe' Deluxe when we owned it. It's very simple, easy to make and easy to expand for a large group. I think chili is the standard bearer for soup in the Midwest. It's hard to find a ma & pa restaurant that doesn't serve it.

At the Cafe' Deluxe we gave an option to add fresh chopped onions and grated cheese on top.

If you like it hotter, add some red cayenne pepper, chopped jalapeno peppers, or go for the throat and add chopped habeneros. (Careful with that in Norwegian company)

(serves 12-16)

2 lbs. ground beef
Salt and fresh ground black pepper
2-28 oz. cans whole tomatoes
2-28 oz. cans beans in chili sauce
2 large onions, diced
2 large green peppers, diced
3 garlic cloves minced
Tomato juice (optional)

Brown ground beef and season with salt and pepper to taste. Drain. Place in large pot. Add whole tomatoes with juice and break up a bit. Add beans, onions, green peppers, and garlic. Bring to a boil and simmer for about ten minutes. If you like your chili thinner, add some tomato juice.

Green Chili

This is ultimately a white bean and chicken broth based soup. And it is fun. Green chiles have such a unique flavor that just blend into and enhance almost any dish you put it into.

(serves 12-16)

- 3 qts. chicken broth
- 2 lbs. lean pork, seasoned with salt and fresh ground black pepper
- 12 green chiles, roasted, deskinned, destemmed, seeded, and diced (or 2 4 oz. cans diced green chiles)
- 1 large red onion, diced
- 3 garlic cloves, minced
- 2-15 oz. cans pinto or white beans, drained

This is just too simple. Cut pork into bite sized pieces. Brown and drain. Put all ingredients in a large pot. Bring to a boil and then simmer for 15 minutes. Serve immediately with some hearty bread.

Chef's note: If you want to thicken this soup, just make a roux. To do this, melt 1/4 lb. butter in large pot on low heat. Add 1 cup of flour. Whisk for 4 minutes or so until it no longer tastes like flour and has a nutty flavor. Add simmering soup to pot and bring to a boil. Soup will thicken immediately.

Mini Meatball Soup

I like to have a lot of fun in the kitchen. We always have a houseful on the weekends. I'm not talking just the kids, their significant others, and their children. It's not unusual for twenty to thirty people to stop by and, of course, they need to eat. Soup is a great way to take care of a crowd. It was fun making this recipe up. I saw something like this on a cooking show, said "that's neat" and here is my version.

- 4 qts. chicken broth
- 1/2 lb. ground beef
- 1/2 lb. ground pork
- 2 eggs
- 1 cup Italian bread crumbs
- 1-2 tsp. Cajun seasoning
- Salt and fresh ground black pepper to taste
- 4 oz. small pasta rings
- 1 lb. 30-40 count fresh shrimp, peeled and deveined
- 2 tbl. butter
- 4 cloves garlic, minced
- 1 onion, diced
- 4 oz. fresh basil, shredded

Pour broth into a large pot. Bring to a simmer. Mix beef, pork, eggs, bread crumbs, cajun seasoning, salt, pepper, and two of the minced garlic cloves. Roll into bite size meatballs. Saute meatballs over medium heat until cooked through. Drain on paper towels. Saute shrimp and remaining garlic in butter for 3-4 minutes and set aside. Add meatballs to simmering broth for 5 minutes. Add pasta for 5 minutes. Add shrimp, onions, and basil and serve immediately.

Oyster Stew for Brenda

At our house, it has been a tradition to make oyster stew on Christmas Eve. Brenda just absolutely loves it. Over the years, I have tweaked and tweaked this recipe. It's been a labor of love. So this is our gift to you. Enjoy it over the holidays with your family or just anytime you are in the mood.

(serves 6-8)

1 qt. oysters
1/4 lb. butter
3 tbl. diced red onion
2 garlic cloves, minced
1/2 celery stalk, minced

1 qt. half and half
1/2 gal. whole milk
Salt and fresh ground black pepper
Oyster crackers

Drain oysters and reserve juice. Melt butter in 2 gallon pot or dutch oven. Add oysters, onion, garlic, and celery. Saute until oysters begin to curl at the edges. Salt and pepper to taste. Add half and half, whole milk and reserved oyster juice. Heat to almost a boil. Adjust seasoning and serve with oyster crackers.

Chicken Noodle Soup

I'm always amazed when I walk through grocery stores and see what people put in their carts. Don't get me wrong, I can be the worst sinner too. Our society has become so fast paced. It's so much easier just to throw in a frozen pizza in the oven and not go the extra effort in preparing something. This soup can be made about in the same time as your frozen pizza and I think your family will appreciate the little extra thoughtfulness/effort. Leftover soup is even better on the next day.

(serves 10-12)

- 3 qts. chicken broth (homemade or store bought)
- 3 cups diced cooked chicken (great use of leftover chicken here)
- 1 small onion, diced
- 2 garlic cloves, minced
- 1 large carrot, peeled
- 8 sage leaves, shredded
- Juice of one lemon
- 2 oz. angel hair pasta broken into thirds
- Salt and fresh ground black pepper

Pour chicken broth into a large pot and bring to a boil. Add chicken, onion, and garlic. Keep at simmer. Grate carrot in and add sage. Add lemon and pasta and simmer 10 minutes. Salt and pepper to taste. Ladle into bowls and be ready for seconds.

Savory Cabbage Soup

This is a great way to use up some leftover ham. Or leave the ham out and go vegetarian. This can easily be an everything but the kitchen sink type soup. Throw in whatever you have laying around for veggies and you can't go too wrong. If you have a couple extra potatoes laying around, just dice them up and throw them in. You get the picture. Enjoy it. It's a great fall and winter soup.

(makes 16-20 servings)

- 2 1/2 qts. chicken broth, homemade or store bought
- 1 1/2 qts. tomato based vegetable juice
- 1 large head of cabbage, cored and chopped
- 1/2 lb. carrots, peeled and chopped
- 1 large onion, chopped
- 4 cloves garlic, minced
- 1 lb. smoked ham, diced
- 2 oz. fresh basil, shredded
- Salt and fresh ground black pepper
- Red pepper flakes (optional)

Pour chicken broth and vegetable juice in a large pot. Add cabbage, carrots, onion, garlic, and ham. Bring to a boil and reduce to a simmer. Simmer until cabbage is tender (about 1/2 hour). Add fresh basil and salt and pepper to taste. You probably will not need any additional salt. If you like it hot, add some red pepper flakes. You'll be back for seconds.

Put a Little Zest in Your Clam Chowder

I have a great friend, Jerry, whom I met when building houses in Madison, Wis. He moved to Seattle and bought a 125 ft. tugboat which he turned into a bunk and breakfast. What a great idea.

For about five years, he would fly Brenda and myself out for a week and I would help build or refurbish a cabin on the tug. One day for lunch, Brenda and I went to Duke's. We had the clam chowder, which is chowder with an attitude. Oh, Boy!! Here's our version.

(serves 6-8)

- 4 strips bacon, diced
- 1 med. red onion, diced
- 3 stalks celery, diced
- 1/4 lb. cooked and diced potatoes
- 4 cups heavy cream
- 1 1/2 cups chopped clams
- 1/3 cup flour
- 1/2 cup half and half
- 3 oz. butter
- 2 1/2 cups clam juice
- 2 cloves garlic, minced
- White, black and cayenne pepper to taste
- 1 tsp. marjoram
- 2 tsp. fresh basil
- 1 tsp. Italian seasoning
- 1/2 tsp. thyme
- 2 bay leaves
- 1/8 cup chopped parsley
- 1/4 tsp. dill

Cook bacon until transparent. Add butter, onions, celery, and all seasonings except dill and parsley. Add flour and cook over low heat 3-4 minutes, stirring constantly. Add dairy products and clam juice. Heat just boiling point. Add clams and potatoes. Slowly bring to a boil 2-3 minutes. Turn off heat. Add dill and parsley to garnish.

Cool as a Cucumber Gazpacho

This is one of Brenda's favorite soups. As soon as the garden kicks in with fresh tomatoes and cucumbers we always whip up a batch. It really is one of those dishes that is better the next day when all the flavors have melded together.

(serves 8)

3 lbs. fresh ripe tomatoes, chopped
3 cucumbers, peeled and diced
2 green peppers, destemmed, seeded and diced
1 large onion, diced
2 jalepenos, destemmed, seeded and minced

3 cloves garlic, minced
1 1/2 cups water
1/2 cup extra virgin olive oil
2/3 cup red wine vinegar
Salt and fresh ground black pepper

Combine 1/2 of all of the vegetables with water and olive oil. Puree in a food processor. In a large bowl, combine puree with remaining vegetables. Add the red wine vinegar and salt and pepper to taste. Cover and refrigerate for at least 2-3 hours, or better yet, overnight.

Dance Like Nobody's Watching

I wanted to create a soup that was infused with some of my favorite flavors. Every ingredient in this soup adds it's own unique taste and the outcome is just out of sight. It certainly didn't last very long at my house. A good rustic bread for dipping brings it all together.

(serves 12-16)

- 4 qts. chicken broth (homemade or store bought)
- 2 lbs. small red potatoes
- 2 lbs. hot Italian sausage links
- 1 red onion, chopped
- 4 cloves garlic, minced
- 4 oz. fresh or frozen green beans, french sliced
- Juice of one lime
- 8 oz. 30-40 count uncooked shrimp, peeled deveined
- 2 oz. fresh basil (about a handful), shredded
- Salt and fresh ground black pepper

Boil potatoes in large pot until just tender. Drain and let cool. In the meantime grill or pan fry sausages. Take off heat and let cool. Dice potatoes and thinly slice sausages. Pour chicken broth in a large pot. Bring to a boil. Add potatoes, sausage, onion, garlic, green beans, and lime juice. Simmer for 5 minutes. Add shrimp and basil. Simmer another 3-4 minutes until shrimp turns pink. Do not overcook or shrimp will become tough. Add salt and pepper to taste and serve immediately. YUMMY!!!

Party Favors

Remember back in the good old days when cocktail parties were really parties? You know, when it was cool to run around with a lamp shade on your head, hors d' oeuvres were a Ritz cracker covered with cheese whiz and a slice of green olive, and the drunkest one at the party drove everyone else home. Ah , the good old days. Come reminisce with us now as we take you back to those golden days. I know! I know! You can see visions of rumaki and crackers with deviled ham spread. And those miniature cocktail meatballs with toothpicks standing tall in a savory barbeque sauce. Maybe a cheeseball or two. And of course, cocktails.

Let's move forward to today and check out how times have changed. Lamp shades are out and the drunkest one at the party is shuttled safely home by somebody sober. But hors d' oeuvres carry on. After all, it is a party and everyone loves to eat. Isn't it wonderful, we have been able stretch our imaginations and bring to the table some really creative dishes. I just love it!!!

So call up your friends and commandeer a cocktail party. Have everybody bring their latest sensation and just marvel, marvel, and marvel about everyone's creation. I always walk away from gatherings like this and am in awe of great new party favors.

Tulip Teacups for Pat

My good friend Pat had a birthday recently and invited us over for dinner. I decided to bring an appetizer plate and came up with the following dish. It takes a little practice to get the prosciutto to wrap like a tulip but the result is definitely great eye candy. You will want to have 6 shot glasses on hand to make teacups.

(makes about 24 appetizers)

8 oz. shredded parmesan cheese
8 oz. paper thin sliced prosciutto
8 oz. cream cheese at room temperature
2 oz. fresh chives
4 oz. sour cream

Juice of one lemon
1/2 lb. 60-80 cooked count shrimp, peeled and deveined
48 fresh chive stalks (about 4" in length)

Preheat oven to 325 degrees. Using a couple cookie sheets, one sheet at a time, make 6 4" circles with the parmesan cheese on sheet. The cheese should just be sprinkled into a circle and not piled on thick. Place in oven and let just melt, 3-4 minutes. While cheese is melting, repeat process. When cheese is just melted, take cookie sheet out of oven. Use a spatula to remove cheese and set over shot glass. Let it fold over to form a cup. Let cool and remove. Repeat process until cheese is used up. Cut prosciutto into pieces just big enough to cover the inside of the cup, and form a tulip, overlapping a bit. In a food processor, add cream cheese, 2 oz. chives, sour cream, lemon, and shrimp. Process until smooth. Fill each tulip cup with this mixture and garnish with 2 chive stalks.

Shrimp Painted Desert

I made this dish for a Valentines party at my neighbors, Carl and Gail. It's my version of a recipe I came across in a great cookbook called *Southwest Tastes* by Ellen Brown. It's a lot of fun to assemble and gives a great presentation. You will need 2 plastic squeeze bottles for this recipe.

(serves 8)

16 Precooked 16 count shrimp, peeled and deveined

White Sauce
- 1/2 cup white wine
- 1 tsp. minced green onion (white part only)
- 2 cups heavy cream
- Salt and white pepper

Red Paint
- 1 tbl. olive oil
- 2 garlic cloves, minced
- 1/2 cup mild red chile powder
- 3/4 cup water

Green Paint
- 3/4 cup olive oil
- 2 garlic cloves, minced
- 4 oz. fresh basil leaves
- Salt and white pepper

White Sauce
Place white wine and onions in a sauce pan. Bring to a boil and reduce by half (about 5-7 minutes). Add cream and cook over low heat until it is reduced to 1 1/2 cups (about 15 minutes). Whisk frequently. Season to taste. Process in a food processor until smooth. Let cool.

Red Paint
Heat oil over medium heat in a saute pan. Saute garlic about 3 minutes to just tender. Add chili powder and water. Blend well. Put in food processor and blend until smooth. Pour into plastic squeeze bottle and refrigerate.

Green Paint
Saute garlic over medium heat in a little olive oil until tender. Add to the rest of the oil and basil in a food processor. Puree and add salt and pepper to taste. Pour into plastic squeeze bottle and refrigerate.

Shrimp Painted Desert
Paint 8 salad plates with white sauce. Take 2 shrimp and make a heart shape at the bottom of each plate. Starting at the top of each plate, make about a 1/2 inch loop design across the top with red paint. Next go below red loops and add green loops. Alternately repeat until about halfway down the plate. Chill until ready to serve. Garnish a basil leaf or two.

Pita Points and Hummus

Talk about the acceptance of multicultural dishes in the Midwest. In Decorah, Iowa, where we live, a rural farming community of 8,000, we have not one, but two restaurants that serve this dish. I think if we could get everyone to sit around the table and share a plate, the possibility of peace in the Mideast may just be attainable.

(serves 8-10)

2 cups cooked or canned and drained chickpeas or garbanzo beans
1 cup tahini
3 garlic cloves, minced
Juice of 2 lemons

Water to moisten
1 tsp. cayenne pepper
Salt and fresh ground black pepper
6 slices pita bread, toasted in the oven

Blend chickpeas, tahini, garlic, lemon, 3-4 tbl. water and cayenne pepper in food processor. If mixture seems a little dry, add a little more water. Salt and pepper to taste. Chill for 1-2 hours. When ready to serve, toast pita bread in oven, Cut each piece into 8 wedges. Spoon some hummus on top of a wedge and you are good to go.

Seafood Cerviche

The acidity of the lime marinade in the dish actually cooks the fish. If adding fish, I like to use firm fish so it doesn't flake when you put a fork to it. I also precook any shrimp that I put in. A cool refreshing treat with little zest to liven up your next get together.

(serves 6)

- 8 oz. precooked shrimp, peeled deveined
- 8 oz. bay scallops
- 8 oz. cleaned squid, cut into bite sized pieces
- 10 limes
- 4 Roma tomatoes, diced
- 1 small red onion, sliced thin
- 2 ripe avocados
- 2 tsp. dried Mexican oregano
- Salt and fresh ground black pepper
- Fresh parsley sprigs

In a 13 x 9 non metallic baking dish, combine seafood. Cover with the juice of 8 limes completely. Add more juice if necessary. Cover and refrigerate for at least 8 hours. Drain. Place in large bowl. Add tomatoes and onion. Cut avocado in half lengthwise all the way around. Twist cut sides and remove pit. Scoop out avocado meat and dice into 1/2 inch pieces. Add with oregano to seafood mixture. Salt and pepper to taste. Plate up and garnish with sprigs.

Green Chile and Black Olive Quesadillas

Here's a dish that is simple and everyone can get involved in the making. Use this recipe as a base and go wild with other ingredients to toss in. (Onions, chopped tomato, chorizo sausage, shrimp, etc.) Line everything up in bowls or plates and let everyone build their own quesadilla and have a hand at cooking them also. Just be careful and keep a close eye on the children.

(serves 4-6)

8-10" flour tortillas
8 oz. shredded Monterey Jack cheese
2- 4 oz. cans diced green chiles

1- 6 oz. can sliced black olives
Salsa
Sour cream

Warm a griddle or large frying pan to low/ medium heat. Place 1 tortilla in pan and spread 1/8 cheese over half. Add some green chile and some black olives. Fold other half over and press edges together. Cook for about 1 minute and flip over. Cook another minute. Remove. Cut into wedges and serve with salsa and sour cream. Repeat process. Remember, if you desire any other fillings, just have them on hand.

Spring Rolls with Chile Hoisin Dipping Sauce

One of my good friends, Bruce, lives in Des Moines, Ia. with his wife, Paula, and their respective children. Bruce has a architectural design company and one thing he always has his designs on is great food. Whenever I'm in town, we sally out to find a different culinary delight. He took me to Anon's, a Vietnamese establishment that served just fabulous spring rolls. Here's my version.

(makes 12 large rolls)

Spring Rolls
- 12-8" spring roll wrappers
- 1/2 lb. cooked shrimp, peeled, deveined, and chopped
- 1 1/4 cups matchstick cut carrots
- 1 cup fresh bean sprouts
- 2 oz. fresh mint, diced
- 2 oz. fresh cilantro, diced
- 12 thin sliced red onion rings

Sauce
- 2 green onions, diced
- 2 tbl. Hoison sauce
- 2 tbl. soy sauce
- Juice of one large lime
- 1/2-1 tsp. red pepper flakes

In a large flat bowl, place four spring roll wrappers in warm water. When softened, take one out and lay on counter. Put a little of each ingredient on the bottom third of wrapper. Fold bottom over. Fold in sides, and roll up. The wrappers are a little fragile, so don't push to hard. Repeat process until all wraps are made. Cover every four with wet paper towels on a plate. Wrap with plastic wrap and chill. For sauce combine all sauce ingredients and chill.

St. Paddy Day Party Eggs

Pat and Kerry have a wonderful St. Patrick's Day party every year. It's a pot luck sort of fling. So hold the green food coloring.

A couple of years ago, I decided to be a little mischievous and liven up the deviled eggs I was bringing with a wee bit of fresh jalapeno peppers. Well, maybe not a wee bit.

And sure and begorin' wouldn't ya know, Kerry had decided to be a wee bit mischievous himself and did the same exact thing. Here's my contribution.

(makes 24 appetizers)

1 dozen large eggs
Mayonnaise
1-2 tbl. prepared yellow mustard
1 tsp. garlic powder
2 jalapeno peppers, deseeded, destemmed and minced fine
Salt and fresh ground black pepper to taste
Paprika
Lettuce

Add eggs to boiling water for 15 minutes. Drain and run cold water over until cooled. Refrigerate 2 hours. Peel. Slice eggs in half the long way. Remove yolks and put a mixing bowl. Add mayonnaise to moisten. Add prepared mustard to taste. Add jalapenos and mix well. Salt and pepper to taste. Cut 1/4 inch tip off of a bottom corner of a gallon freezer bag. Place egg mixture in, and using like a pastry bag, fill egg whites. Sprinkle paprika over. Shred lettuce and spread over a large serving plate. Top with eggs and refrigerate until ready to serve.

Lettuce Wrapped Shrimp Tacos

Look Mom, no taco shell!! A great little appetizer to put on the menu when throwing a build your own party. You serve the shrimp cold with a Greek sauce and a Mexican salsa. Now that's fusion. It's a shrimp salad in your hand. It's also very light, all veggie (except shrimp, of course) and keeps saying just let me make one more.

2 lbs. 50-60 count cooked cold shrimp, shelled and deveined
3-4 avocados, peeled, diced, and soaked in juice of 1 lemon
2 heads Romaine lettuce, bottom removed

Greek Sauce

- 2 small cucumbers, peeled, seeded, and diced
- 1 1/4 cups plain yogurt
- 2 tbl. olive oil
- 4 cloves garlic, minced
- Juice of 1 lemon
- 2 tsp. dried dill weed
- Salt and fresh ground black pepper

Salsa

- 2 medium tomatoes, diced
- 1/2 medium onion, diced
- 1 green pepper, diced
- 4 garlic cloves, minced
- 3 deseeded jalapenos, minced
- Juice of 1 lime
- Salt
- Fresh ground black pepper

Mix all Greek sauce ingredients together and salt and pepper to taste. Refrigerate for 2 hours. Do the same with salsa. When ready to serve, have guests take a lettuce leaf and lay some shrimp in it. Cover with some Greek sauce and add some salsa. Garnish with avocado and eat away.

Buffalo Wings, Won't You Come Out Tonight?

Our good friends, Jeff and Cindy and daughter Lindsey, live in Berea, Ohio. When we get to visit, we head to the Oriole restaurant and bar and Jeff and I always order their wings. At first, they served wings mild to atomic. We got an order of hot and then tried the atomic. Well, neither of us thought atomic was that hot, so I went back to the kitchen and kiddingly told the cooks they should add a little heat to their wings.

Next time we went back, super atomic was on the menu, and the wings were smoking. With tears in our eyes after only a couple, we knew we'd met our match.

5 lbs. chicken wings
Salt and fresh ground black pepper
32 oz. peanut or corn oil

1/4 lb. butter
10 tbl. Louisiana hot sauce
2 tbl. white or red wine vinegar

Cut small ends off wings and discard. Cut remaining wing into 2 pieces at joint. Wash and pat dry. Salt and pepper to taste. In a deep heavy bottomed skillet or pot bring oil to 375 degrees. Use a candy thermometer to check temperature. You do not want to burn the oil. Fry wings in batches until golden brown, about 3 minutes or so. Place on paper towels to drain. Melt butter and add hot sauce and vinegar. When all the wings are done, put in a large serving bowl and pour sauce over and mix well. If you like it hotter, add some more hot sauce. I think you'll like this one.

Very Veggie Party Pizza

Oh my! Oh my! Here we have a different pizza pie. A horse of another color, one might say. Toppings are limited only to the extent of one's imagination. Be creative and make two or three different types for your next get together. Your guests will love you for it.

(makes 2- 12 inch pizzas)

- 2 Precooked 12 inch pizza crusts, homemade or store bought
- 3- 8 oz. packages cream cheese at room temperature
- 4 garlic cloves, minced
- 2- 12 oz. bottles chili sauce
- 2 tbl. fresh ground horseradish
- Juice of 1 lemon
- 1 cup finely diced broccoli tops
- 1/2 cup finely chopped carrots
- 1/2 red pepper, finely diced
- 1/2 red onion, finely diced

If you are making homemade pizza crusts, see page 104. Pierce crusts with a fork and bake for 10 or so minutes or until crusts are golden. Cool. Place pizza crusts on 12 inch pizza pans. Use a food processor or mixer and mix cream cheese and garlic well. Divide in half and spread on each crust. Mix chili sauce, horseradish, and lemon juice together. Spread evenly over cream cheese. Top with veggies. Cover with plastic wrap and refrigerate for at least two hours. Cut with a pizza cutter in small pieces when ready to serve. It got great raves at my house when we served it up. Have fun!!!

Midwest Americana

We are a nation undivided. We just can't seem to agree on anything. It is agreed, however, that there seems to be an overabundance of plastic pink flamingos on the lawns in the Midwest. Not to mention ceramic deer and frogs, creatures such as eagles and bears hand sculpted by chain saws out of huge logs, and, of course, gazing balls. And let us not forget the occasional plywood grandmother caricature in a flowered dress bent over in the garden.

This phenomenon is running rampantly across all ethnic lines it seems. The shanty Irish have lost their hold, as if they ever had any, on lawn ornamentation. (No offense to be taken here, I've always been a little shanty Irish myself, it tends to give a wonderful perspective on human nature.) I think it's just great. Doesn't it bring out the child in all of us? A little nostalgia of when we were all young. The world was our playground. Every moment could lead to a wonderful new discovery. Our minds were open slates. We breathed in the excitement of our fascinating and unfolding glimpses of life at every turn we took.

Then the age of reason kicked in. Our bubble burst. Good-bye youthful innocence. Welcome to reality.

But all is not lost. We still have our memories. And when those memories involve family and food, the comfort and security of home come into play. Those great festive holidays and get-togethers where the aromas of wonderful food permeated the air. In the kitchen with Mom or Dad, licking the frosting spoon or eating fresh mashed potatoes with turkey and gravy surrounded by love. How could it get any better?

Probably it is time to thank Mom and Dad for those great memories. Probably time also to pick a couple of new pink flamingos for the lawn.

Herb Roasted Turkey with Gerda and Jim's Homemade Stuffing

We have Thanksgiving at our house every year. We have both my side and Brenda's side of the family over, friends and people who we know that don't have a place to go. We always have a huge ham and a couple of 20# plus turkeys. Believe me, I have cooked turkeys in many different forms over the last twenty five years. From deep fried cajun style, brining, marinated with citrus, etc. This year we made one with the following recipe. The stuffing recipe is what my mom, Gerda, always made while I was growing up. Of course, I can never leave anything alone, so in the years that I've taken on the host job for Thanksgiving, the stuffing has evolved to the following recipe. If you want to leave out the sausage, the stuffing will still be sensational!

(serves 12-16)

- 1 16-18 lb turkey, fresh or thawed
- 1/4 lb. butter
- 2 oz. fresh sage leaves
- 1-1 lb. loaf white cottage bread
- 1-1 lb. loaf whole wheat bread
- 8 oz. fresh mushrooms, sliced
- 6 celery stalks, chopped fine
- 1 large onion, diced
- 4 garlic cloves, minced
- 1 lb. cooked ground pork sausage
- 4 oz. slivered almonds
- Ground dried sage
- Salt and fresh ground black pepper
- 3 large eggs, whisked
- 32 oz. chicken broth

Turkey

Preheat oven to 450 degrees. Remove giblets and neck from turkey. Wash and pat turkey dry. Remove any lingering feathers and/or fat. Gently put your hand under skin over turkey breast on one side and loosen. Be careful not to pierce skin. Cut the butter into small slices. Place of the butter and sage under skin and over breast. Repeat on the other side. Place in oven in roasting pan breast side down and bake for 20 minutes. Take out and turn breast side up. Reduce oven temperature to 350 degrees. Roast turkey for 15-20 minutes per pound until it reaches an internal temperature of 165 degrees and juices run clear. Baste with melted butter or turkey juices every 30 minutes or so. If turkey gets to brown towards the end tent with aluminum foil. Take out and allow turkey to rest 10 minutes before carving.

Stuffing

Toast bread and cut into 1/2 inch pieces. In a large mixing bowl, combine toast, mushrooms, celery, onions, garlic, and sausage. Lightly season with sage, salt and pepper. Toss and season again. Repeat twice more. Add eggs and mix thoroughly. Slowly add chicken broth and mix well. Bake in oven in a large casserole dish along with turkey for 1 1/2 to 2 hours until the middle of stuffing is at 165 degrees.

Norwegian Meatballs with Mashed Potatoes and Gravy

My son Conor has a great friend Jens. Conor and Jens were inseparable for years. Jens spent many a night at our house and is like a son to me as well. He called up one day and said that he and his girlfriend Anna were going to get married and asked if we would cater it for them. I was truly honored. We decided on a crazy menu with two main courses.

Get this, we served chicken creole for one main dish and Norwegian meatballs with mashed potatoes and gravy for the other. We'd also made up some yukon gold garlic mashed potatoes and ended up serving twice as much of the garlic than the regular. I guess we have come a long ways in Spicing up Norway.

(serves 8)

Meatballs

- 6 slices white bread
- 1 cup hot milk
- 1 lb. lean ground beef
- 1 lb. ground pork
- 1/2 tsp. nutmeg
- 1/2 tsp. fresh ground black pepper
- 1/4 tsp. allspice
- 3/4 cup diced onion
- 2 1/2 tsp. salt

Gravy

- 8 tbl. butter
- 8 tbl. all purpose flour
- 5 cups boiling beef broth

Mashed Potatoes

- 2 1/2 lbs. peeled russet potatoes, cut into small pieces
- 3-4 tbl. butter
- Milk

Preheat oven to 350 degrees. Soak bread in hot milk in a large bowl. Add all meatball ingredients and mix thoroughly. Roll meatball mixture into 1" balls. Brown meatballs in a little oil in a large heavy skillet. Place with a slotted spoon in a 9 x 15 casserole dish.

Melt butter in a large sauce pan over med/low heat. Add flour and stir constantly for 4 minutes or until flour mixture gets bubbly. Add broth and stir until it thickens. Pour over meatballs and save any extra. Bake 30 minutes.

Place potatoes in boiling salted water in a large sauce pan. Boil for 25-30 minutes until tender. Drain. Add butter and mash. Add milk a little at a time until you reach your desired texture. Dish up some meatballs and add some gravy to your serving of potatoes.

Don't Let Your Meat Loaf

I like to make meatloaf on the bold side of life. With gusto. The combination of beef and pork work well together and I like to add the eggs in as a good binder. Traditionally, catsup is used as a topping, but I like to be a little different. So I've added some horseradish and lemon juice which essentially is shrimp cocktail sauce, but it also works well here.

(serves 8)

1 1/2 lbs. ground beef
1 1/2 lbs. ground pork
2 eggs
1 cup Italian bread crumbs
1 green pepper, diced (optional)
1/2 red onion, diced

2 garlic cloves, minced
2 tsp. salt
1 tsp. fresh ground black pepper
1/2 cup catsup
1 tbl. fresh ground horseradish
1 tsp. lemon juice

Preheat oven to 350 degrees. Combine beef, pork, and eggs. Mix thoroughly in a large bowl. Add bread crumbs, onion, garlic, salt and pepper. Mix thoroughly as well. Shape into 2 same-sized loaves. Place in a 9 x 15 lightly greased baking dish. Bake for twenty minutes. In the meantime, mix catsup, horseradish, and lemon. Brush over top of meat loaves and bake another 25-30 minutes until meat is no longer pink inside.

Corned Beef and Cabbage with Parsley Potatoes

We're ending up back at our favorite watering hole "Your Place" because it's St. Patrick's Day. Tom and Theresa put on a wonderful free feed for all of their customers. I cook up the corned beef using a technique given to me by Don, who with his wife Louise ran the Family Store, a small meat market/grocery for years. They have both passed on, but the recipe lives on and I'm sharing it with you.

(serves 6-8)

1-2 1/2-3 lb. corned beef
3 lbs. new small red potatoes
1/2 cup fresh diced parsley
1/4 cup butter

1 large head cabbage
1/4 cup butter
Salt fresh ground black pepper to taste

Preheat oven to 325 degrees. Place a wire rack over a 9 x 15 baking dish and add 1/2 inch water. Arrange corned beef fat side up on top of rack in center. Bake for 2 1/2 -3 hours until tender. Pull and let stand 10 minutes. About 30 minutes before corned beef is ready, boil potatoes in salt water until just tender, about 20-25 minutes. Drain and put in large skillet. Set aside and keep warm. At the same time, have a steamer or large pot of water boiling. Quarter cabbage and cut out core. Either steam or boil cabbage until tender, 20-30 minutes. Drain, add 1/4 cup butter and toss. Keep warm. When corned beef is out of oven, add parsley and 1/4 lb. butter to potatoes. Warm over medium heat and toss. Slice corned beef very thin after removing the fat. Serve with cabbage and potatoes.

Garlic Studded Prime Rib with Duchess Potatoes

I save this dish for special occasions, like when heads of state come to town or we're entertaining the Pope. Seriously, this ends up being for special occasions, mostly driven by cost. I always ask my butcher to cut out the rib bones. I stud it with the garlic slices and then tie the rib bones back on with butcher's twine. It really adds flavor to the meat and pan drippings for Au Jus.

(serves 8)

- 5-6 lbs. standing beef rib roast with rib bones cut away
- 3-4 garlic cloves
- 8 baking potatoes
- 8 tbl. sour cream
- 2 tbl. butter
- 2 oz. Parmesan cheese
- Milk
- Salt
- Nutmeg

Preheat oven to 350 degrees. Using a small paring knife make slits all around the roast. Slice garlic cloves into thin slices and insert in slits. Tie rib bones back on. Bake in oven for 2 1/4 hours for medium rare at center. (140 degrees at center). Tent with aluminum foil the last hour. Wash potatoes and pierce with a fork in several places. Bake along with rib roast about an hour or until potatoes are soft. Pull out and let cool a little. Slice off the tops the long way about an 1/4 inch down. Scoop out potato insides. Place in mixing bowl with sour cream, butter and cheese. Beat with electric mixer until smooth, adding a little milk to moisten if necessary. Put mixture in pastry bag or gallon plastic storage bag with corner cut out and refill skins looping in the potato mixture. Sprinkle with nutmeg. Reheat for 15 minutes.

Chicken Vesuvio

This is a Chicago restaurant inspired recipe that my good chef friend Nina decided to make for a crowd at our house one day. We are making it as I am writing. Simply easy to prepare and simply just delicious.

(serves 4)

- 4 split chicken breast halves, skin and bone on
- 1 1/2 lbs. baking potatoes
- Dried leaf oregano
- Salt
- Fresh ground black pepper
- 3 whole cloves garlic, peeled
- 1/2 cup extra virgin olive oil
- 1 cup dry white wine
- Fresh parsley

Preheat oven to 375 degrees. Wash and pat dry chicken. Scrub potatoes and cut into wedges. Sprinkle chicken on both sides with oregano, salt, and pepper. Repeat with the potatoes. Heat olive oil in a large heavy bottomed skillet to about 300 degrees. This will not take long. Olive oil has a low burning point so keep your eye on it. Toss garlic cloves in and saute for 2 minutes. Remove with a slotted spoon and discard. This will infuse the oil with a garlic aroma. Brown chicken breasts on both sides and place in a large baking dish. Repeat with potatoes. Bake for 30 minutes until when you pierce the chicken with a knife, the juices run clear. Meanwhile, Add white wine to the empty skillet over heat and scrape all of the bits and pieces off the bottom. Stir and set aside until chicken and potatoes are ready. Arrange chicken on a serving platter and pour wine sauce over. Bon Appetit !!!

Stuffed Green Peppers

Try these for a little change of pace when the peppers are ripe in the garden or at any time for that matter. A little basic tomato sauce (page 102) tops them off nicely. A couple of side dishes and you're ready to go.

(serves 4)

- 4 large green peppers
- 1 1/2 lb. ground Italian sausage, mild or hot
- 1 cup cooked rice
- 4-5 button mushrooms, diced
- 1/2 cup onion, diced
- 3-4 garlic cloves, minced
- 2 1/2 cups homemade tomato sauce or store-bought spaghetti sauce

Preheat oven to 325 degrees. Remove top from green peppers. Remove interior stems and seeds. In a medium mixing bowl, combine Italian sausage, cooked rice, diced mushrooms, onions, garlic and 1 cup tomato sauce. Mix well. Use a wooden spoon and carefully stuff a pepper, making sure that you don't pack it too tightly. Place in small baking dish that will hold the four peppers. If you have leftover stuffing mix, just put around peppers in bottom of dish. Bake for 75-90 minutes until sausage is no longer pink in middle. Pull and let rest for 5 minutes. Meanwhile, heat remaining tomato sauce in a small sauce pan on stove. Place a pepper on each plate and ladle some sauce over. Serve some good garlic bread and a side salad. Just another great dimension using simple ingredients.

Ginger Almond Cornish Game Hens and Fresh Red Potatoes

Boy, I like this recipe. Have a little party. Everyone gets their own bird and they are just succulent. If you want to serve an up-scale supper fairly inexpensively, here's the one. Maybe add some fresh green beans with red onions and bacon. MMM,MMM,MMM.

(serves 4)

- 4 Cornish game hens
- 2 peeled cloves garlic
- 1 cup slivered almonds
- 1 tbl. fresh grated ginger root
- 1 tsp. salt
- 1 tsp. paprika
- 1/2 tsp. fresh ground black pepper
- 1/4 tsp. cumin
- 1/4 cup melted butter
- 2 lbs. fresh small red potatoes (washed and scrubbed)

Preheat oven to 375 degrees. Remove neck and heart/ gizzard packages from birds. Save hearts and gizzards, if desired, and add to baking dish. Rinse birds under cold water and remove any fat. Pat dry and set aside. Combine garlic, almonds, ginger, salt, paprika, pepper, and cumin in a food processor and chop fine. Put mixture on a large plate. Brush birds one by one with melted butter and roll in mixture. Place in 9 x 15 non-greased baking dish breast side up. Arrange potatoes around birds. Bake 60 minutes or so until juices from birds run clear. Your guests will just marvel.

Thin Sliced Pork Chops and Easy Salad

Need something quick for supper? The Cajun seasoning lends the pork chops a wonderful flavor. You can make this up in 10-15 minutes. Pan fry the chops as you assemble the salad. Make sure, as always, that pork is cooked thoroughly.

(serves 2)

- 2-4 thin (1/4 inch thick) sliced fresh pork chops
- 2 tbl. corn oil
- Cajun seasoning
- 1/2 head of your favorite lettuce, shredded
- 1/4 onion, sliced thin
- 12 pitted green olives
- 12 red grapes, seedless
- 1/2 cucumber, sliced
- 1 med. tomato, cored and wedged
- 3 tbl. extra virgin olive oil
- 2 tbl. lemon juice
- 1 tbl. red wine vinegar
- 1 tsp. crushed dried oregano
- Salt and fresh ground black pepper

Pan fry pork chops over med/high heat 3-4 minutes a side until thoroughly cooked. Toss lettuce, onion, olives, grapes, cucumber, and tomato. Briskly mix olive oil, lemon juice, red wine vinegar, oregano, and salt and pepper to taste. Pour over salad mixture and serve immediately with pork chops.

Brenda's Goulash and Jim's Garlic Bread

Talk about a hot combination. No, not Jim and Brenda. Brenda has been making her goulash for years. Everyone loves it. I like it best served right away. Use some of Jim's garlic bread to sop up the succulent juices, and then have seconds.

(serves 6-8)

6 oz. elbow macaroni
1 lb. lean ground beef or turkey
1 onion, chopped
1 red pepper, diced
1/2 green pepper, diced
2 cloves garlic, minced
1 tsp. salt

1/2 tsp. fresh ground black pepper
1/4 tsp. red pepper flakes (optional)
1-28 oz. can diced tomatoes
1-15 oz. can whole tomatoes
1 loaf rustic french bread
1/4 lb. butter
2 cloves garlic, minced

Cook macaroni noodles according to package directions. Drain. Brown ground beef/turkey and add onion, peppers, garlic, salt, black and red pepper while browning. Drain and add to macaroni in a large pot. Add tomatoes. Bring to a boil and simmer 10-15 minutes. Slice french bread in two the long way. Melt butter and add 2 cloves minced garlic in small pot. Brush over bread and bake for 12-15 minutes at 275 degrees while goulash is simmering. Cut up bread and serve immediately with goulash.

Just Desserts

"Let them eat cake" cried Marie Antoinette after she heard there wasn't enough bread for the peasants to go around. Let's see. That means the peasants would be able to have their cake and eat it too!

Now that's what I call "Just Desserts."

And for all of you aficionados of the sweeter things in life, it's time to step up to the cake plate. The Sugar Plum Fairies are in town, you're the home team, and it's the bottom of the ninth. As you eye the field of confection, you know time has come to put the frosting on the cake. Ever so boldly, you stroke out a home run. Your fans scream with delight as you share with them a slice of your stupendous hit.

"Is this heaven?' asked Shoeless Joe Jackson of Ray Kinsella in The Field of Dreams. "No, this is Iowa" Ray replied. It's also back to reality for us. Baking is as much science as it is anything. If you are making a pot of chile, you can toss in different amounts of ingredients and still have a great dish. Change the quantity amount in Mom's angel food cake and you are likely to have a disaster on your hands. If the recipe calls for a level teaspoon of baking powder, that's what you put in, not a heaping teaspoon.

Okay, with that in mind, let's do dessert. Be creative. Follow directions. And we too can have our "Just Desserts."

Charlie's Tiramisu

My nephew, Charlie, shared his Tiramisu recipe with me. He was 14 when he started making it. What a treat! A great dessert chef in the making perhaps. We didn't have any lady fingers available, so we substituted short bread cookies and the result was still spectacular. Thanks for a great recipe, Charlie!

- 3 cups espresso
- 1/2 cup Kahlua
- 1 pkg. ladyfinger cookies (You may not use them all)
- 5 egg whites, 4 egg yolks (both pasteurized)
- 1/2 cup sugar
- 14-16 oz. marscapone cheese
- 3/4 tbl. vanilla
- cocoa

Chef's note: You will want to have a glass serving bowl to present this dish in.

Mix espresso and Kahlua in a bowl and chill. Beat egg whites until they peak in a mixer. In a separate mixing bowl, add egg yolks, sugar, and vanilla. Mix until creamy yellow. Blend cheese into the yolk mixture. Dip enough ladyfingers into coffee mixture one by one to cover bottom of the serving bowl. Be careful to just let them absorb some coffee but not get too wet. Add a layer of egg/cheese mix. Sprinkle on a little cocoa and keep repeating process. Chill 2-3 hours. Simply divine!

Rømmegrøt Bars

It is time to give my good Norwegian friends due respect. Here is a wonderful treat that Darlene shared with me. It is a recipe her mom passed down to her. Her husband, Jeff, brought them to work one day. Everyone wanted the recipe. I decided to share it as well. It is simply delicious. Those Norwegians surprise you at times.

Pastry Dough

- 1 cup milk
- 1/4 cup sugar
- 1/2 tsp. salt
- 1 pkg. dry active yeast
- 2 tbl. warm water (105-110 degrees F)
- 3/8 stick butter, melted
- 1 egg yolk
- 3 cups all purpose flour

Filling

- 2-8 oz. pkgs. cream cheese
- 1 cup sugar
- 1 egg yolk, whisked
- 1 tsp. vanilla

Topping

- 1/3 cup sugar
- Cinnamon

Scald milk in a quart pot. Add sugar and salt. Cool to about 105-110 degrees. In your mixer bowl add yeast to the warm water and dissolve. Add milk, butter, egg yolk, and 1 1/2 cups flour. Beat until smooth, scraping the sides as necessary to mix well (1 1/2 minutes or so). Add remaining flour and stir in by hand until well incorporated. Cover with plastic wrap and refrigerate for 3 hours or more.

Preheat oven to 350 degrees. Put all filling ingredients in mixing bowl. Beat on medium until smooth. Grease the bottom of a 11x17 baking dish. Take dough out and divide into two. Roll 1/2 dough very thin into a 11x17 rectangle. You might have to flour your rolling surface or rolling pin a little bit. Place rolled out dough in bottom of baking dish. Spread filling over dough evenly. Roll out remaining dough and lay on top. Sprinkle 1/3 cup sugar and enough cinnamon to please the eye on top. Bake for 20-25 minutes until top begins to turn golden at the edges. Take out and place on a cooling rack. When cooled down to room temperature cut into bars.

Chef's note: If you are in a hurry, substitute two large or three regular packages of store bought crescent rolls for the dough. Enjoy!

Strawberry and Rhubarb Pie

Mom and Dad always had a huge garden. Rhubarb always came in first. Mom would cut it up and freeze it. When strawberries came in, it was time for some serious blending of tart and sweet. Talk about Ying Yang! It's a great marriage of opposites. I like a lattice crust on this pie for a nice presentation. My good friend Clayton from work and his grandmother, Judy, helped me out on this. Both with rhubarb in the fall when I couldn't find any, and Judy's recipe which I consorted with to come up with this version. Thanks for all the help, Clayton and Judy!!

(serves 6-7)

Dough
(makes 2-10" circles)
- 2 cups white flour
- 1 tsp. salt
- 2/3 cup cold shortening
- 2 tbl. cold butter
- 4+ tbl cold water

Filling
- 3 cups chopped rhubarb
- 3 cups sliced strawberries
- 1 1/3 cups white sugar
- 1/4 cup cornstarch
- Sprinkle of cinnamon
- 2 egg whites, beaten

Make dough by cutting half of the shortening and butter into the flour. Work it by hand or use a pastry blender until it gets grainy. Add the rest of the shortening and butter. Work to pea size. Add water and mix gently by hand into a dough. If it is too dry, add a teaspoon of water. On a floured surface, roll into 2- 10" circles. Place one circle into a 9" pie pan. Make sure sides are covered. Set other circle aside.

Preheat oven to 425 degrees. Combine rhubarb, strawberries, sugar, and cornstarch in a medium sized mixing bowl. Sprinkle with cinnamon. Toss and sprinkle again. Put mixture on top of the pie dough in the pan. Cut the remaining pie dough into 1/2 strips. Create a lattice topping by laying 6 strips spaced apart across pie in one direction. Lay one strip crosswise over the 6 strips at 1 inch in from the end of the pie. Gently fold the 6 strips back to the one you just put a strip in crosswise. An inch from the folded back strips, lay that strip. Lay the 6 strips over the new strip and take out to the end of the pie. Repeat process until pie is covered with a lattice topping. Brush on enough egg white mixture to wet latticework. Bake at 425 degrees for 15 minutes on a cooking sheet. It should start to brown at this point. Reduce heat to 375 degrees. Bake another 50-60 minutes. Cool on a cooling rack. Place in refrigerator for 4 hours or better to set up. If you cut the pie when it is still hot, you will get a lot of juice. Goes great with ice cream!!!

Peanut Butter Cream Pie

I worked with Don for many years. We became great friends. His passion for food lies more towards baking and desserts. Actually, Don and his wife Carol downright love to make desserts. They are always trying a new treat. I asked Don if he had made any neat desserts lately, so he shared this with me. Well done, Don and Carol!

Crust

- 1 1/4 cups graham cracker crumbs
- 1/4 cup granulated sugar
- 6 tbl. melted butter

Filling

- 11 oz. cream cheese (1-8 oz. pkg. and 1-3 oz. pkg) room temperature
- 1/2 cup creamy peanut butter
- 1 cup powdered sugar
- 1/4 cup 1/2 and 1/2
- 10 oz. whipping cream
- Shaved semi-sweet chocolate

Combine graham cracker crumbs and sugar. Add melted butter and mix thoroughly. Press into the bottom and sides of a 9 inch pie plate. Chill for 1 hour. In a mixer, beat cream cheese and peanut butter until smooth. Add powdered sugar and 1/2 and 1/2. Beat once more until smooth. Whip whipping cream until it becomes stiff with soft peaks. Slowly and carefully fold into peanut butter mixture. Spoon into crust. Sprinkle with shaved chocolate. Chill again. This is ABSOLUTELY DELICIOUS!!!!!!

Wedding Carrot Cake

Brenda and I got married in 1979. We had a small wedding with about 100 guests. We made all the food except the cake. Brenda asked Karla to do that. I called Karla to see if she would share the recipe. She laughed and said it was a Cafe Deluxe recipe she used and I needed to call Amy to see if she still had it. She did and was happy to pass it on to everybody. Thanks a lot, Karla and Amy!!!

Cake
- 1 cup oil 2 cups sugar
- 1/2 tsp. vanilla
- 1/4 cup buttermilk
- 4 eggs, beaten
- 2 cups grated carrot
- 2 cups flour
- 2 tsp. cinnamon
- 2 tsp. salt
- 1 1/2 tsp. baking powder
- 1/4 tsp. nutmeg

Frosting
- 1 1/2 cups confectioner's sugar
- 6 oz. cream cheese
- 3 tbl. cream
- 2 tsp. vanilla
- 1 tsp. cinnamon

Cake
Preheat oven to 350 degrees. In a mixing bowl, beat oil and sugar well. Add vanilla, buttermilk, eggs, and carrot. Put the remaining dry ingredients in another mixing bowl and slowly add wet ingredients to dry. Mix into a smooth batter. Pour batter in a 9 x 12 baking dish. Bake for about 1/2 hour. When a toothpick is inserted in center of cake and comes out clean, cake is ready to come out of the oven. Place on cooling rack.

Frosting
Beat cream cheese and cream until soft and whipped. Beat in sugar slowly. Add in vanilla and cinnamon and mix well. Frost cake while it is still warm.

Chef's note: If you place frosting over boiling water for 10 or so minutes, it will cancel out the raw taste of the sugar.

Have You Tried a Kolache?

The small towns of Spillville and Protivin, not far from where I live, have a rich Czech heritage. Kolaches rule there. Every home baker has his/her favorite method of making them and they all seem to be wonderful. Essentially, they are egg pastry dough with fillings like poppy-seed, prunes, cherries and other fruits. Just mouth-watering. A friend of mine, Randy, supplies homegrown fresh farm eggs to some of the premier kolache bakers in the area. His wife, Laura, has had the opportunity to be present and assist these bakers from time to time. Here is a recipe she shared with me. Thanks a lot, Randy and Laura!!!

(makes 2 dozen)

- 2 egg yolks + 1 egg
- 1/4 cup sugar
- 1/2 cup shortening (your choice)
- 1 tsp. salt
- 1 tsp. vanilla
- A pinch of mace
- 1/4 cup dry potatoes + warm water to make 1/2 cup
- 2 pkgs. Rapid Rise Yeast
- 1 cup very warm milk
- 3 1/2 cups flour (start with 3 1/4, then add more if needed)
- 8 oz. fruit (Like prunes, apricots, or raspberries)
- Water to just cover
- 1/2 cup sugar
- 1 tbl. butter

In a mixer bowl, beat yolks and egg well. Add sugar, shortening, salt, vanilla, and mace. Beat again. Add potatoes and mix. Add yeast and beat well. Add warm milk and 2 cups flour. Beat for 3 minutes. Add rest of flour slowly until a ball is slightly formed. You may not use it all. Place in a greased bowl. Grease top lightly. Cover and let rise until double. Punch down and work with fingers 18-20 times. Grease again, cover and let rise until double.

While dough is rising, make filling. Boil the fruit with water about 15 minutes until fruit is tender. Drain and mash. Add sugar and butter. Blend well.

Rub in flour on a coarse cloth and put dough on that. Let rest for a few minutes. Roll out or pat into a 10 x 16 inch rectangle about 1/4-1/2 inch thick. Let rest 5 minutes. Cut into 24 squares. Put a heaping tsp. of filling in the center of a square. Bring opposing corners of the square to meet in center. Repeat with the other 2 corners. You now have a kolache. Place a baking sheet and make the up the remaining 23. Cover and let rise until double. Bake in a preheated oven at 400 degrees for 8-10 minutes until light brown. Check the underneath. If too light, place on a lower rack for a little bit. Check often or they can get too dark. Take and place each on a cloth to cool.

Chef's note: You can buy prepared fillings in your grocery store baking department if you prefer to not make filling.

Streuselkuchen

Here is a favorite of mine from growing up. Mom made it a lot. It is very simple to make. If you have a child who likes to help in the kitchen, he or she can help roll out the dough. Try sprinkling a little cinnamon on for a pleasant change of taste.

1 cup milk
3 tbl. butter
1 package yeast
2 tbl. sugar
3 cups unbleached white flour
2 tsp. salt
1 egg white

Topping

1 cup flour
1/2 cup sugar
1/2 cup butter, cut into 1/4 inch pieces

Heat milk and butter over low heat until butter just melts. Add to standing mixer bowl that has a dough hook. Add yeast and sugar. When mixture becomes bubbly, turn mixer on low and slowly add flour. Increase mixer speed to medium after dough begins to form. Add salt and egg white. Mix about 10 minutes, until dough is no longer sticky to touch. Knead by hand for 2 minutes. Form into a ball and place into a large oiled bowl. Turn dough in oil to coat entirely. Cover with plastic wrap. Let rise until doubled.

While dough is rising, make topping. Combine flour, sugar, and butter in mixer. Beat together until the mixture becomes crumbly. Preheat oven to 350 degrees. Spread dough by hand over a large baking sheet. Cover with crumb mixture and bake 25-30 minutes until just turning light brown. Cool and cut into 3 inch squares.

Poppyseed Cake with White Vanilla Frosting

Another from my mom's collection which I really like. Great to serve at your afternoon coffee or just about anytime. I wonder how many poppies it takes to make one cake?

Cake
- 3/4 cup poppyseeds
- 3/4 cup milk
- 3/4 cup shortening
- 1 1/2 cups sugar
- 2 1/2 cups all purpose white flour
- 3 tsp. baking powder
- 1/4 tsp. salt
- 1 tsp. vanilla
- 4 egg whites

Frosting
- 1/4 cup butter
- 2 cups powdered sugar
- 1 tsp. vanilla
- 2 tsp. milk

Soak poppyseeds overnight in 3/4 cup of milk. In a mixing bowl add sugar to shortening and beat to a creamy consistency. Alternately add dry ingredients and the milk and poppyseed mixture. Add vanilla. Beat egg whites to a peak and fold into batter. Bake in a preheated oven at 375 degrees for 25 minutes in a 13 x 9 baking. Let cool completely. Make frosting by completely creaming frosting. Frost when cake is cool.

Strawberries and Irish Cream Delight

My great friend Jane, a pastry chef in her own right, brought a chocolate torte with fresh raspberries to a five couple rotating dinner club we do about every two months. It was a two person participation dish as one of my other great friends, Leon, her husband, and she put it together. Talk about the crescendo of the meal!! It inspired me to make this recipe. Thanks, Jane and Leon.

Base

- 1 1/2 cups unbleached white flour
- 1/4 cup sugar
- 3 tbl. unsweetened cocoa
- 1/2 tsp. salt
- 1 1/2 sticks butter cut into 1/4 inch pieces
- 1/2 cup butterscotch morsels
- 3 egg yolks

Topping

- 4 tbl. Irish Cream liqueur
- 1 tsp. gelatin
- 1/2 cup butterscotch morsels
- 3 oz. chopped bittersweet chocolate
- 1 3/4 cups heavy whipping cream
- 1 lb. fresh strawberries, sliced

Combine flour sugar, cocoa, and salt in a food processor. Process with butter until it becomes crumbly. Add butterscotch morsels and egg yolks. Process until it starts to look like dough. Shape into a ball. Spray the bottom of a 9 inch spring pan (side removed). Flatten dough on pan bottom. A sheet of wax paper and a rolling pin can help here. Cover and refrigerate for 1 hour. Bake in a preheated oven at 375 degrees for about 25-30 minutes or until dough is dry on top. Cool to room temperature.

Put 2 tbl. Irish Cream in a small sauce pan. Top with gelatin. Let it set up 4-5 minutes. Add 3/4 cup cream. Heat over low heat, stirring frequently. When bubbles form on the side, turn off heat. Add butterscotch morsels and chocolate. Stir until smooth. Cool also to room temperature. Beat remaining cream and Irish Cream in a mixer to a firm set. Add to butterscotch and chocolate and gently mix. Put spring pan side around bottom of pan. Add remaining mixture on top of baked crust. Put in refrigerator for one hour. Place strawberry slices in concentric circles on top. Refrigerate overnight.

Chef's note: Shaved white chocolate can add a little more zest over the top of the strawberry slices.

My Favorite Irish Joke

An Irish priest and a Rabbi get into a car accident. They both get out of their cars and stumble over to the side of the road.

The Rabbi says, "Oy vey! What a wreck!" The priest asks him, "Are you all right, Rabbi?" The Rabbi responds, "Just a little shaken."

The priest pulls a flask of whiskey from his coat and says, "Here, drink some of this it will calm your nerves." The Rabbi takes the flask and drinks it down and says, "Well, what are we going to tell the police?"

"Well," the priest says, "I don't know what your aft' to be tellin' them. But I'll be tellin' them I wasn't the one drinkin'."

What Goes on in the Cornfield, Stays in the Cornfield

Really? You know with all those ears out there you'd think somebody's tassels would be talking. And there is a lot to be talking about. Just speak with the good folks in Mitchell, South Dakota. Here we find an epic saga of pure corn. I'm sure we have all made up a list of two thousand three hundred forty seven and a half things to do before we die. Well a trip to the Corn Palace in Mitchell is a must on that list. It is utterly a"maize"ing. A block long edifice covered with murals made up mostly of different colored, sliced in half, ears of corn. Each year a new theme is depicted in these murals and what's left of the last year's murals is taken down. I say what's left because this is truly the world's largest bird feeder.

The high school team is known as the "Kernels" and the local radio station is "KORN." Every year Mitchell has a week long festival dedicated to what else but "CORN." Boy, those South Dakotans sure know how to have fun!

When I told my friend Pam that I was writing a cookbook called Midwest Corn Fusion, she said I absolutely had to include a chapter on corn. I said "Pam, I'm all ears." I'm also convinced that she must hail from South Dakota. All corniness aside I hope you have a little fun with this chapter. Enjoy!!

Sweet Corn with Lime and Red Pepper Butter

In Iowa, starting in June, the sweet corn trucks start arriving and setting up at convenient store parking lots. Pickups are loaded to the max with ears of corn and everybody is buying it by the dozen. I love sitting out on the deck, relaxing after work, and shucking a few ears. Try this with our lime/pepper butter. What a great new dimension.

(serves 6)

1 dozen ears fresh sweet corn
1/4 lb. butter

1 fresh lime
1/4-1/2 tsp. cayenne pepper

Fire up the barbeque grill to medium heat. While it is warming up, husk the sweet corn. Break off end stem and make sure to pick off all of the tassel strands as possible. Next, melt butter in a small sauce pan. Add about a tbl. of fresh lime juice and the cayenne pepper. Stir and turn off heat. Place ears of corn on grill and keep a close eye on them. You will want to keep turning the ears until kernels are browned on all sides. Try to keep blackening to a minimum, although you probably will get a little. Take off grill and pass the lime pepper butter around. Yahoo!

Chef's note: When you buy sweet corn, make sure to open husks and look at the ears. Kernels should be full and plump and go to the end of the ear.

Green Chile Cornbread

A good friend, Don, brought a version of this to a potluck at our house. He made his with canned jalepenos. Hoo-Hoo, it was great. This recipe is toned down considerably. However, the secret to great cornbread is moisture. So you don't want to overcook it. This even meets Fawn's approval for hotness, and she has a hard time with most of my spicy dishes.

(serves 8)

- 1 1/2 cups buttermilk
- 1 4 oz. can green chiles or 4 green chiles (roasted, destemmed, deseeded and chopped)
- 1 large white onion, diced
- 2 cloves garlic, minced
- 1 cup yellow cornmeal
- 1 cup white flour
- 2 tsp. sugar
- 1 tbl. baking soda
- 1 tsp. baking powder
- 1 tsp. salt
- 2 large eggs
- 1 cup sharp cheddar cheese, grated

Preheat oven to 400 degrees. Put buttermilk, chiles, onion, and garlic in saucepan and cook over low heat for 5-6 minutes, stirring often. Let cool for 15 minutes. Mix cornmeal, flour, sugar, baking soda and powder and salt in a large bowl. Beat eggs and add cheese. Fold into cornmeal mixture and mix until just blended. Try not to overdo the mixing so the batter stays light. Pour into a greased 1 1/2 quart baking dish and bake for 40-45 minutes or until golden brown. Test with a toothpick. Cornbread is ready when toothpick comes out clean from center.

Mark's Corn Chowder

At the Cafe' Deluxe we always had a least two soups going on. Chili was always one and then we would make up one or two more everyday. Mark, who was our morning manager and cook, made a wonderful corn chowder. I called him up at his restaurant "La Rana" and asked if he would share it with us. He laughed and said "Mac, you aren't going believe this, but that is what I'm making right now for the lunch crowd." Here is a version I'm sure you will enjoy.

(serves 10-12)

- 2 lbs. potatoes
- 1 medium red onion, diced
- 4 tbl. olive oil
- 4 tbl. all purpose flour
- 4 cups buttermilk
- 4 cups whole milk
- 2 tsp. fresh ground black pepper
- 1 1/2 tsp. salt
- 2 cups fresh or frozen sweet corn
- 1/2 lb. bacon, diced
- 1/2 red pepper, diced

Peel and dice potatoes. Boil until just tender. Mash one half of potatoes. Saute onion in olive oil until translucent in a large stock pot. Add flour and whisk over medium heat 3 minutes. Add milk and remaining ingredients. Slowly bring to a boil and turn off immediately. Make sure to keep stirring almost constantly, to keep milk from scalding on the bottom of pot. Adjust seasoning to taste. Thanks Mark!!!

Corn and Shrimp Bisque

Let's take it to another level. The sweetness of corn and shrimp just marry each other. Obviously fresh shrimp is the way to go if it is available. This can easily be the main course for your dinner table. It certainly is on the rich side. If you would like it a little tamer, substitute some 1 or 2% milk for the buttermilk.

(serves 8-12)

- 1 lb. 40-50 count cooked shrimp, peeled and deveined
- 4 tbl. butter
- 4 tbl. flour
- 4 cups chicken broth
- 4 cups buttermilk
- 8 oz. bottled clam juice
- 1/2 large onion, diced
- 3 cloves garlic, minced
- 16 oz. can diced tomatoes
- 1 celery stalk, diced
- 2 cups fresh or frozen sweet corn
- Salt and fresh ground black pepper

Chop the shrimp and set aside. In a large pot or dutch oven, melt butter at medium heat. Add flour and cook, stirring constantly for 3 minutes. Add chicken broth, buttermilk, and clam juice. Bring to a boil and reduce heat to a simmer. Add onion, garlic, tomatoes, and celery. Simmer for 7-8 minutes. Add corn and chopped shrimp. Seasoning with salt and pepper to your taste.

Corn Bread Pot Pie

Here's a little twist on pot pie using our green chile corn bread batter as the topping instead of a traditional pastry crust. It's delicious. Use the recipe on its own or if you have gravy and some meat or poultry dish leftovers you can experiment and create an easy/fun way to use up those great remnants.

(serves 8)

1/2 recipe Green Chile Cornbread batter (page 187)
4 cups diced cooked chicken
16 oz. mixed frozen vegetables
1 medium onion, diced
1 cup diced carrots
1/4 lb. butter
1/2 cup flour
4 cups chicken broth

Place chicken, frozen vegetables, onion, and carrots in an 11x17 baking dish. In a medium sauce pan melt butter. Over low/ medium heat, add flour and whisk continually for 4-5 minutes. It should start to taste nutty and no longer like flour. Add chicken broth and bring to a boil. This will thicken into a gravy. Pour over chicken and veggies. Mix well. Pour corn bread batter over. Bake for 35-45 minutes in a preheated oven at 400 degrees until a toothpick comes out clear from corn bread. This is good stuff!!!

Basic Fresh Corn Tortillas

Fresh tortillas are like manna from heaven. Although you can make these using a rolling pin, if you can afford to buy a tortilla press for around $15, it works much more smoothly and will last a life time. I made these the first time in Mexico at a small cantina that actually was just the cook's house. Talk about a lesson in humility. Rolling out by hand wasn't as easy as it looked.

(makes 16 6" tortillas)

2 cups corn flour
1 1/8 cups water

peanut or corn oil

In a mixing bowl, combine flour and water and form into a firm ball of dough. It should hold together but not be wet. If it is crumbly, just add a little water. If it is too wet, just add a little more flour. Break in half. Then break in half again. Repeat until you have 16 pieces. Form into balls and cover with a wet towel. Bring a griddle or a heavy bottomed skillet to high heat on your stove with no oil. Cut a gallon freezer bag down the sides. Place in tortilla press so dough will be in between plastic. Place dough in center of press and press down. You now have a tortilla. If you don't have a press, place dough between plastic and press with a heavy book or use a rolling pin. Gently remove from plastic and place in skillet. Fry on each side 15-30 seconds until cooked through. Place on a plate and cover to keep warm. If you want to make tostada shells or tortilla chips, heat 1 inch of oil in a heavy bottomed skillet to 350 degrees. For tortilla chips, cut into 6-8 wedges per tortilla. Fry single tortillas or a batch of wedges for about 30-60 seconds until golden brown. Place on paper towels and add salt if desired.

Corn, Red Pepper, and Black Bean Salsa

This can be served either as a relish or side dish. If fresh sweet corn is available, I like to roast it on the grill and cut the kernels off to use. Roast the pepper at the same time. If you prepare it this way, you'll probably need 3-4 large ears of corn for 2 cups. Don't worry if you have too much. Just add it in. The more the merrier.

- 2 cups, roasted on the grill, sweet corn kernels
- 3 red peppers roasted on the grill, deskinned, deseeded, and diced
- 2-15 oz. cans black beans, drained and rinsed
- 1 medium onion, diced
- 3 cloves garlic, minced
- 4-5 jalapenos, destemmed, deseeded, and minced
- Juice of 2 limes
- Salt and fresh ground black pepper

Roast sweet corn and red peppers on the grill. Keep turning. You don't want to burn the corn. Nice and browned is perfect. This really brings out the natural sugar in the corn. Pull and let cool. The peppers will take about 8-10 minutes longer. When peppers are blackened and blistering pull off grill and put in a paper bag for 15 minutes. Slice off kernels of corn. Pull off skins of peppers, deseed and dice. Put corn, peppers beans , onions, garlic, and jalapenos in a serving bowl. Add lime juice. Salt and pepper to taste. My 2 year old grandson, August, just can't get enough of this.

Dana's Chile Corn Bread Salad

I was working on this book one sunny afternoon and our friends Dana and Clair stopped by. We, of course, started discussing food. Dana said she had a corn bread salad recipe she wanted to share with me. Boy, am I glad she did. What fun!! Thanks, Dana.

(serves 12)

- 1 recipe Green Chile Corn Bread (see page 187), cooled
- 1 cup mayonnaise
- 1 cup sour cream
- 1 pkg. ranch salad dressing mix
- 2 cans pinto beans, drained and rinsed
- 16 oz. fresh or frozen whole kernel corn
- 3 med. tomatoes, chopped
- 1 large green pepper, diced
- 1 cup chopped green onions
- 10 strips cooked bacon, crumbled
- 2 cups cheddar cheese, shredded

In a small bowl, combine mayonnaise, sour cream, and ranch dressing. Set aside. In a large bowl, crumble the corn bread. Add beans, corn, tomatoes, green pepper, green onions, bacon and cheese. Mix. Stir mayonnaise into mixture. Cover and refrigerate for at least 2 hours.

A Little Corny Casserole

This is one of those dishes you can have fun with by using your imagination and ingredients you think might inspire this dish to higher levels. A little red and green pepper for color, fresh mushrooms, and cooked Italian sausage for additional flavor. Your ingenuity can make great different creations using the same basic recipe.

(serves 8)

- 2 cups fresh off the cob or frozen sweet corn
- 2 cups cooked ground Italian sausage
- 2 cups grated cheddar cheese
- 6 oz. fresh sliced white button mushrooms
- 1/2 red pepper in 1/4 x 1 inch slices
- 1/2 green pepper in 1/4 x 1 inch slices
- 1/2 red onion, diced
- 3 cloves garlic, minced
- Salt and fresh ground black pepper
- 16 oz. sour cream
- Crushed saltine crackers

Preheat oven to 325 degrees. In a greased 9 x 13 baking dish, add corn, sausage, cheese, mushrooms, peppers, onion, and garlic. Mix together well. Salt and pepper to taste while mixing. Use a spatula and spread sour cream over the top. Bake for 45 minutes. Pull out of oven and sprinkle crackers over the top. Bake for an additional 20 minutes.

Jimmy Crack Corn Cakes

You probably haven't found these on a restaurant menu lately. A fun little treat that stands on it's own, but also can stand the presence of great accompaniments. You can serve these up for breakfast with some maple syrup or honey for toppings. They will also make a great side dish at your next BBQ.

(12-16 cakes)

- 1 cup cornmeal
- 1 cup pancake mix or cake flour
- 1 tsp. baking powder
- 2 eggs
- 1 1/2 cups fresh or frozen sweet corn kernels
- 1 cup buttermilk
- 2 tbl. corn oil
- 2 tbl. chopped fresh chives
- 1/4 tsp. salt

Mix the dry ingredients (cornmeal, flour, and baking powder) in a medium sized mixing bowl. In another bowl beat eggs and add corn, milk, oil, chives, and salt. Mix well. Fold into dry ingredients gently. You just want to get the mixture wet all the way through. No need to over work it. Lightly oil a large skillet or pancake griddle. Drop about 3 tablespoons of batter on hot surface for each cake. Fry like a pancake, turning once to cook each side. The kids will absolutely love them and love to help to make them.

Chef's note: For fresh corn, husk a 2-3 large ears. Remove all corn hairs. Use a paring knife and shave kernels off ear.

My Favorite Irish Joke

An Irishman walks into the pub and orders three pints of Guinness. He asks that they be brought over to him at the table. The Irishman drinks the pints one at a time and then leaves. This routine goes on for about two months.

Finally, the bartender asks why the Irishman has the three pints. "Well'" he says, " The first pint is for me brudder in Amerikay and the second is for me brudder in England." The bartender nods in agreement and tells the lads at the bar who have witnessed the comings and goings for the two months.

Several weeks latter, the Irishman enters the pub and orders two pints. As the bartender walks up to the table with a pint in each hand, he says. "If you don't mind my asking, have you lost one of your brother?" The Irishman pauses for a second, sees the two pints and says, "Oh forsakes no, I quit drinking this week!"

Index

A

Appetizers
    Buffalo Wings, Won't You Come Out Tonight? **158**
    Green Chile and Black Olive Quesadillas **154**
    Lettuce Wrapped Shrimp Tacos **157**
    Pita Points and Hummus **152**
    Seafood Cerviche **153**
    Shrimp Painted Desert **151**
    Spring Rolls with Chile Hoisin Dipping Sauce **155**
    St. Paddy Day Party Eggs **156**
    Tulip Teacups for Pat **150**
    Very Veggie Party Pizza **159**
Asparagus and Red Onion with Dijon Parmesan Sauce **47**

B

Beans
    Green Salsa, Tortilla and Black Bean Casserole **134**
    Marvelous Drunken Beans and Grilled Sausage Delight **123**
    Pita Points and Hummus **152**
Beef
    American-Italian Spaghetti **108**
    Basic Chili **139**
    Beef and Horseradish Salad **53**
    Blue Cheese and Red Onion Hamburger **31**
    Bowtie Delight **135**
    Brenda's Goulash and Jim's Garlic Bread **171**
    Corned Beef and Cabbage with Parsley Potatoes **165**
    Don't Let Your Meat Loaf **164**
    Easy Lasagna/Easy Garlic Bread **103**
    Easy, So Easy Rouladan **43**
    Fire in the Hole Sirloin Wrap **23**
    Garlic Studded Prime Rib with Duchess Potatoes **166**
    Marinated Ribeyes with Fresh Grilled Sweet Corn and Chile Butter **98**
    Mini Meatball Soup **141**
    Norwegian Meatballs with Mashed Potatoes and Gravy **163**

Beer-batter Pancakes **120**
Bratwurst
    "It's the Wurst" **115**
    Mac's Cajun Sizzlers **15**

C

Cheese
    Beer and Cheese Fondue **118**
    Blue Cheese and Red Onion Hamburger **31**
    Cheese Enchiladas **36**
    Evening Omelettes with Brenda **32**
    Garlic Cheese Biscuits **33**
    Green Chile and Jack Cheese Wontons with Mustard Dipping Sauce **41**
    Homemade Mac and Cheese **30**
    Parmesan Crisps **28**
    Wisconsin Beer Cheese Soup **29**
    Quiche Lorraine **34**
    Very Grilled Cheese Sandwiches and Fresh Tomato Soup **37**
Corn
    A Little Corny Casserole **194**
    Basic Fresh Corn Tortillas **191**
    Corn and Shrimp Bisque **189**
    Corn Bread Pot Pie **190**
    Corn, Red Pepper, and Black Bean Salsa **192**
    Dana's Chile Corn Bread Salad **193**
    Green Chile Cornbread **187**
    Jimmy Crack Corn Cakes **195**
    Mark's Corn Chowder **188**
    Sweet Corn with Lime and Red Pepper Butter **186**

D

Desserts
    Charlie's Tiramisu **174**
    Have You Tried a Kolache? **179**
    Peanut Butter Cream Pie **177**
    Poppyseed Cakewith White Vanilla Frosting **181**
    Rømmegrøt Bars **175**
    Strawberries and Irish Cream Delight **182**
    Strawberry and Rhubarb Pie **176**
    Streuselkuchen **180**
    Wedding Carrot Cake **178**
Dressings
    Beef and Horseradish Salad **53**
    Pasta Salad with Homemade Green Goddess

Dressing *59*
South of the Winneshiek County Border Salad with Fresh Salsa Dressing *54*
Watercress Rehearsal Salad *55*

E

Eggs
Evening Omelettes with Brenda *32*
Ham & Egg Brunch Casserole *131*
Mushroom and Scallion Omelet *73*
Quiche Lorraine *34*
St. Paddy Day Party Eggs *156*

F

Fish/Seafood
Bruce's Grilled Oysters in the Shell *94*
Classic Tuna Casserole with a Little Umph *127*
Erik's Smoked Chicken\Erik's Blackened Salmon *96*
Fish Tacos *17*
Oyster Stew for Brenda *142*
Put a Little Zest in Your Clam Chowder *145*
Seafood Cerviche *153*
Seafood Manicotti *106*
Shanon's Premium Beer-battered Fish *116*
Tuna Stuffed Tomatoes *82*
Shrimp
Cappellini *109*
Corn and Shrimp Bisque *189*
Dance Like Nobody's Watching *147*
Lettuce Wrapped Shrimp Tacos *157*
Prosciutto Wrapped Shrimp (Devils on Horseback) *93*
Seafood Cerviche *153*
Shrimp Creole *6*
Shrimp Diablo *22*
Shrimp Fettucine for Esther *111*
Shrimp Painted Desert *151*
Shrimp Pizza *105*
Shrimp Remoulade *40*
Spring Rolls with Chile Hoisin Dipping Sauce *155*
Tulip Teacups for Pat *150*

G

Green Chiles
Green Chile and Black Olive Quesadillas *154*
Green Chile and Jack Cheese Wontons with Mustard Dipping Sauce *41*
Green Chile Cornbread *187*
Green Chili *140*
Lamb Stew with Jalapenos and Green Chiles *20*
Pork and Green Chile Empanadas *11*

L

Lamb
Guinness and Lamb Irish Stew *114*
Lamb Stew with Jalapenos and Green Chiles *20*
Mac's Twisted Greek Lamb Casserole *129*

M

Mushrooms
Chicken Marsala *72*
Morel and Green Chile Soup *66*
Mushroom and Red Onion Stroganoff *70*
Mushroom and Scallion Omelet *73*
Mushroom Turkey Kabobs and Darlene's Golden Rice *75*
Mushrooms in White Wine *69*
Portabella Pizzettes *67*
Sauteed Morels with Garlic *74*
Sauteed Mushroom Pizza *71*
Stuffed Mushrooms *68*
Mustard
Asparagus and Red Onion with Dijon Parmesan Sauce *47*
Bacon and Spinach Salad with Mustard Dressing *45*
Chicken Breast with Mango Mustard Salsa *49*
Easy, So Easy Rouladan *43*
Fresh Pretzels with Mustard Green Onion Dip *42*
Green Chile and Jack Cheese Wontons with Mustard Dipping Sauce *41*
Honey Mustard Crusted Pork Loin with Black Raspberry Jam *46*
Mustard Glazed Baked Ham *44*
Sauteed Turkey Breast with Basil and Creole Mustard Cream *48*
Shrimp Remoulade *40*

P

Pasta
American-Italian Spaghetti *108*
Baked Spaghetti and Basil Meatballs *133*

Bowtie Delight **135**
Brenda's Goulash and Jim's Garlic Bread **171**
Cappellini **109**
Chicken Cacciatori **107**
Easy Lasagna/Easy Garlic Bread **103**
Morgan's Fresh Out of the Garden Summertime Pasta **57**
Mushroom and Red Onion Stroganoff **70**
Pasta Salad with Homemade Green Goddess Dressing **59**
Seafood Manicotti **106**
Shrimp Fettucine for Esther **111**

Pizza
   Pizza Time **104**
   Shrimp Pizza **105**
   Very Veggie Party Pizza **159**

Pork
   A Little Corny Casserole **194**
   Bacon and Spinach Salad with Mustard Dressing **45**
   Baked Spaghetti and Basil Meatballs **133**
   Chicken and Sausage Gumbo **16**
   Country-style Pork Ribs with Beer Barbeque Sauce **121**
   Dance Like Nobody's Watching **147**
   Don't Let Your Meat Loaf **164**
   Easy Lasagna/Easy Garlic Bread **103**
   Easy, So Easy Rouladan **43**
   Fresh Green Beans with Red Onions and Bacon **85**
   Green Chili **140**
   Grilled Pork Chops and Bavarian Beer Sauce with a **119**
   Ham & Egg Brunch Casserole **131**
   Honey Mustard Crusted Pork Loin with Black Raspberry Jam **46**
   Kansas City Style Back Baby Ribs **91**
   Mac's Country Style Ribs **95**
   Marvelous Drunken Beans and Grilled Sausage Delight **123**
   Mini Meatball Soup **141**
   Mushroom and Red Onion Stroganoff **70**
   Mustard Glazed Baked Ham **44**
   Norwegian Meatballs with Mashed Potatoes and Gravy **163**
   Pizza Time **104**
   Pork and Green Chile Empanadas **19**
   Portabella Pizzettes **67**
   Prosciutto Wrapped Shrimp (Devils on Horseback) **93**
   Savory Cabbage Soup **144**
   Scalloped Potatoes and Ham **126**
   Steamed Prosciutto Asparagus **80**
   Stuffed Green Peppers **168**
   Thin Sliced Pork Chops and Easy Salad **170**
   Tulip Teacups for Pat **150**

Potatoes
   Corned Beef and Cabbage with Parsley Potatoes **165**
   Garlic Studded Prime Rib with Duchess Potatoes **166**
   Gerda's Potato Salad **84**
   Ginger Almond Cornish Game Hens and Fresh Red Potatoes **169**
   Grilled Garlic Lime Chicken with Aluminum Foil Fresh Potatoes **97**
   New Potatoes and Creamed Peas **86**
   Norwegian Meatballs with Mashed Potatoes and Gravy **163**
   Potatoes O'Brien Hash Brown Casserole **132**
   Roasted Garlic and Chive Smashed Potatoes **79**
   Scalloped Potatoes and Ham **126**

Poultry
   Buffalo Wings, Won't You Come Out Tonight? **158**
   Chicken and Sausage Gumbo **16**
   Chicken with 40 Cloves of Garlic **21**
   Chicken Breast with Mango Mustard Salsa **49**
   Chicken Cacciatori **107**
   Chicken Marsala **72**
   Chicken Noodle Soup **143**
   Chicken Vesuvio **167**
   Erik's Smoked Chicken\Erik's Blackened Salmon **96**
   Garlic Beer Fried Chicken **117**
   Ginger Almond Cornish Game Hens and Fresh Red Potatoes **169**
   Grilled Garlic Lime Chicken with Aluminum Foil Fresh Potatoes **97**
   Jim's BBQ Chicken Wings **90**
   Not Just Your Average Drunken Chicken **122**
   South of the Winneshiek County Border Salad with Fresh Salsa Dressing **54**
   Teriyaki Lime Wings **92**

R

Red Chile
   Red Chile Sauce/Salsa Verde **24**
Rice
   Here's the Beef with Wild Rice **128**

S

Salads
- Bacon and Spinach Salad with Mustard Dressing *45*
- Beef and Horseradish Salad *53*
- Brenda's Bountiful Brunch Salad *60*
- Dana's Chile Corn Bread Salad *193*
- Gerda's Potato Salad *84*
- Hail to Ceaser Salad *52*
- Heavenly Coleslaw *61*
- Melon and Fruit Salad *58*
- Morgan's Fresh Out of the Garden Summertime Pasta *57*
- Pasta Salad with Homemade Green Goddess Dressing *59*
- South of the Winneshiek County Border Salad with Fresh Salsa Dressing *54*
- Spinach and Feta Cheese with Spicy Andouille Sauce *56*
- Waldorf Salad *62*
- Watercress Rehearsal Salad *55*

Salsa
- Chicken Breast with Mango Mustard Salsa *49*
- Corn, Red Pepper, and Black Bean Salsa *192*
- Fresh Salsa & Chips *18*
- Red Chile Sauce/Salsa Verde *24*
- Green Salsa, Tortilla and Black Bean Casserole *134*
- South of the Winneshiek County Border Salad with Fresh Salsa Dressing *54*

Sauces
- Baked Cabbage Rolls with Spicy Tomato Sauce *130*
- Basic Red Sauce *102*
- Country-style Pork Ribs with Beer Barbeque Sauce *121*
- Grilled Pork Chops and Bavarian Beer Sauce with a Spaetzle Side *119*
- Italian Gravy *110*

Soup
- Basic Chili *139*
- Chicken Noodle Soup *143*
- Cool as a Cucumber Gazpacho *146*
- Corn and Shrimp Bisque *189*
- Dance Like Nobody's Watching *147*
- Green Chili *140*
- Mark's Corn Chowder *188*
- Mini Meatball Soup *141*
- Oyster Stew for Brenda *142*
- Put a Little Zest in Your Clam Chowder *145*
- Savory Cabbage Soup *144*
- Tortilla Soup *138*

T

Tomatoes
- Mozzarella, Tomato & Basil Bruschetta *35*
- Tuna Stuffed Tomatoes *82*
- Very Grilled Cheese Sandwiches and Fresh Tomato Soup *37*

Turkey
- Brenda's Goulash and Jim's Garlic Bread *171*
- Herb Roasted Turkey with Gerda and Jim's Homemade Stuffing *162*
- Mushroom Turkey Kabobs and Darlene's Golden Rice *75*
- Sauteed Turkey Breast with Basil and Creole Mustard Cream *48*

V

Vegetables
- Baked Acorn Squash *81*
- Baked Cabbage Rolls with Spicy Tomato Sauce *130*
- Brenda's Fresh Dressed Cucumbers and Onions *87*
- Cool as a Cucumber Gazpacho *146*
- Fresh Green Beans with Red Onions and Bacon *85*
- Grilled Zuchinni Creole *83*
- Kohlrabi and Sugar Snap Pea Stir Fry *78*
- New Potatoes and Creamed Peas *86*
- Roasted Garlic and Chive Smashed Potatoes *79*
- Savory Cabbage Soup *144*
- Steamed Prosciutto Asparagus *80*
- Stuffed Green Peppers *168*
- Very Veggie Party Pizza *159*

My Favorite Irish Joke

At the end of his sermon Father O'Briain turned to his listeners and said: "Now, let me ask you. Which of you thinks truly he is bound for Paradise? Would you please stand?"

He was pleased to note that nearly all of his parishioners stood up. "That's good," he exclaimed. "But now, let me ask you. Which of you thinks he is bound for Hell? Would you stand?"

After a few seconds, Jock Burke slowly got to his feet, and remained standing as the priest eyed him with sadness.

Afterwards, as the worshippers filed out, Father O'Briain pulled Jock aside and asked him, "Now, Jock, what is it that makes you fear you're bound for Hell?" To which he responded, "O, Father, I have no fear for my own outcome, but I did feel sorry for you standing up there all by yourself."

My Favorite Irish Joke

Mahoney's wife has to go out of town for the day on a business trip. The last thing she says to her husband is to not go out to the bar in her absence.

As soon as the wife is gone he heads down to Clancy's Pub. After spending most of the day there he decides he'd better get back on home. He gets up from the bar takes a few steps and falls flat on his face. Gets up, takes a few more steps and again, falls flat on his face. All the way home for three blocks its up down up down until he finally makes it home.

 Just after he gets in the house his wife shows up. She walks in the door just as the phone was ringing. She answers it and hangs up after a short conversations. She looks at Mahoney and says, "So you went to Clancy's Pub after all did ya?"

"Well yes dear," said Mahoney, "But how did you know?"

" That's was the barman on the phone calling to say you left your wheel chair there."